Patrick Biedenkapp

PILOT
PATRICK

D1086943

Patrick Biedenkapp

PILOT PATRICK

My glamorously unglamorous life as a jet-set pilot

Bibliographical information from the German National Library:
The German National Library (Deutsche Nationalbibliothek) has recorded this publication in the Deutsche Nationalbibliografie [electronic resource]. Detailed bibliographical information can be found online at http://d-nb.de.

All the stories told in this book are true, but, for privacy reasons, the names of some people and companies have been replaced by pseudonyms, and places and other characteristics have also been changed.

The pictures are from the author's private archive.

For questions or suggestions:
info@rivaverlag.de

1. edition 2020
© 2020 by riva Verlag, an imprint of Muenchner Verlagsgruppe GmbH
Nymphenburger Straße 86
D-80636 Munich
Tel.: 089 651285-0
Fax: 089 652096

Published in Germany in 2020 by riva Verlag, an imprint of Muenchner Verlagsgruppe GmbH, Munich, Germany, as *Pilot Patrick. Mein glamourös-unglamouröses Leben als Jetset-Pilot* by Patrick Biedenkapp.
All rights reserved.

With the collaboration of: Peter Peschke
Translation: Emily Plank
Proofreading: Sylvia Goulding, Diana Vowles
Type-setting: bookwise GmbH, Munich
Cover Design: Marc-Torben Fischer
This book was produced by print on demand.

ISBN Print 978-3-7423-1723-0
ISBN E-Book (PDF) 978-3-7453-1410-6
ISBN E-Book (EPUB, Mobi) 978-3-7453-1411-3

For more information on the publisher, visit:
www.rivaverlag.de
Please also read about our other publishing houses at www.m-vg.de

CONTENT

CHAPTER

GLAMOUR FOR ONE, PLEASE—A TOTALLY "NORMAL" FIRST DAY OF WORK

I had certainly imagined the whole glamour thing to be very different.

Pilot for a private jet airline—it was a job that promised new adventures every single day. Insights into the life of the rich and the beautiful, of the stars and starlets: Brad Pitt and Angelina Jolie, Tom Ford or Karl Lagerfeld would have me fly them to Nice, London, or Paris. New encounters with the jet set every single day, a veritable *Who's Who* of society—and even if I were just their pilot, it would definitely be exciting and always new. This, roughly, is how I imagined my first job after completing the training.

Beautiful, high-quality things have always had an almost magical appeal to me, and in private aviation, that much was certain, I would meet the people who could afford such things. Because if you have sufficient cash to hire a plane and jet from one continent to another, for a weekend of shopping, glamour will also find its place in your life in other ways. The less varied humdrum work at one of the many scheduled flight providers was rather less appealing to me at the time. Instead, I preferred to fly "the celebrities" while getting a little taste of their world. It would somehow be very sexy, that first job of mine, I was sure of that.

So, my first duty was . . . pretty sobering. It had been a few weeks since I had signed my employment contract with a Berlin-based private aviation company. That's when the waiting game started—initially, waiting to finally have my license issued by the relevant authority. Then, having received this, waiting to be included in the new roster. Finally—unexpected and all of a sudden—the day arrived, at long last. I was woken by a call on my cell phone at 6:30 a.m.; a first officer had gone sick and an immediate replacement needed to be found. How soon could I get to the airport? I decided to wing it. With little planning or organization, I threw whatever I could lay my hands on into my suitcase. I hadn't been told how long I would be away, so I didn't know what I was going to need. I quickly ironed my uniform—only to spend the whole trip to the airport trying to remember if I had turned the iron off. I'm sure that's a worry many people have in those kinds of moments. It's baseless, of course—it's just that we have too much time to think about it. And that doesn't necessarily change once you're onboard the plane. But this time, I would be in the cockpit, so would soon be otherwise occupied. (My house was still standing when I got back; I had turned the iron off.)

I met the rest of the crew at the General Aviation Terminal (GAT) of Berlin Schönefeld airport. There were three of us: the captain, a Polish stewardess, and me. I had seen the stewardess maneuvering a fully loaded discount store shopping cart along the tarmac on my way to the plane. She had obviously been tasked to procure drinks and other stuff for the flight. Yet, despite the champagne bottles I spotted in the cart, there wasn't a whole lot of glamour going on. Even the hangar outside which the plane was parked looked pretty cheerless, though the aircraft itself, a Cessna Citation XLS, was worth well over US$11 million.

The captain seemed like the kind of guy who believed jumping in the deep end was the best way to learn how to swim: He cut straight to the chase to explain PF ("pilot flying") to me. As you might expect, this term means that I would be the one controlling the plane while he monitored. I knew this would be part of my "line training," where you learn all the specific flight operation procedures, but was nevertheless quite surprised to discover it would be happening on my very first flight. The captain would of course instruct and assist me where necessary, as he was aware it was my first duty for the company. But it was still all a little unexpected, and felt like a giant leap of faith. I was both proud and nervous.

We would be flying from Berlin to Zurich—initially without passengers, as per the plan. This made the "stage fright" a little more bearable. I did, of course, know what I had to do once I took my seat on the right-hand side of the cockpit. I had practiced the procedures over and over again during my training. But it was still all unfamiliar to me. I wasn't sitting in the good ol' flight simulator, where, if in doubt, I could just press "Pause." It wasn't a case of going through the correct emergency procedures as we usually did in training. It was a regular flight from A to B, which was something I had so far—if ever—only practiced without any passengers or crew. Plus, we were late; our VIP client would soon be landing in Zurich, which was now our destination. Private aviation is not an industry where providers can afford to be tardy. In short: It was time to put my skills to the test. There was no room for error, and I was suitably tense. But I was managing okay in the cockpit. All the checks went to plan, and the plane responded to my actions and commands. Finally, ladies and gentlemen, we reached our scheduled altitude and set off toward Zurich.

Short superstars and mountains of meatballs

Once at Zurich airport, we prepared the plane for our actual flight order. Abundant catering was ready and waiting at the GAT. But our client, a rich Polish woman—or should I say: the daughter of a very rich Pole—, kept us waiting. Oh well; at least I got to have my first celeb sighting: A lady with a long blonde mane, climbing rather awkwardly out of another private plane, turned out to be Colombian pop star Shakira. "Can she not walk?" I wondered. At first glance, you could have been forgiven for thinking she wasn't totally sober, given the way she staggered across the tarmac to the terminal. But, looking a little closer, I saw that her main problem was most probably the giant platforms affixed to the bottom of her shoes (which easily elevated her above the 5'6" mark, even though she's really only 5'1"). Shakira may not quite have been up with the latest shoe fashion, but still: It was thanks to her that I got a brief glimpse of a world-famous star on my first day of work. I was also shocked at the piles of luggage she was traveling with; a seemingly endless trail of suitcases and bags was being hauled out behind her. The plane was also a Cessna Citation XLS, so I was able to get an idea of what I could expect in future—because loading and unloading luggage was the crew's job.

We were ready for our onward flight to Warsaw. The only person missing was our client. Along with the captain and stewardess, I waited for the lady who would be providing me with my first glamorous assignment. The catering alone looked promising. It would have been enough for the entire crew. Mountains of attractive appetizers, including meatballs. Plus, canapés, a selection of salads, and a whole bunch of fruit cut into mini works of art. All for just one person and a 90-minute flight. I had to restrain myself from grabbing some. The champagne, which had also been carted onboard in crates, was of course already a no-go for us.

Finally, a call came from OPS ("Flight Operations"): The flight had been canceled for that day. While I was the one on my first duty, it was the client who had committed the rookie mistake that resulted in the cancelation: When booking her connecting flight from Zurich, she had done so for the same day as her flight from New York—without taking into account the fact that this first flight was an overnight one lasting more than eight hours. So, the connecting flight wouldn't be happening until the following day. She had booked us twenty-four hours early. While we were waiting here, she was probably still supervising the staff in her New York penthouse, making sure they were packing her bags correctly. (As everyone knows, rich people always live in penthouses and have their bags packed for them. In reality, I actually have no clue what Madam's living arrangements were.)

The 6:30 a.m. phone call, the panicked bag-packing and unnecessarily hasty dash, the flight to Zurich—it had all been for nothing. I then had someone ask me, in all seriousness, if I could help dispose of the catering. I'm always happy to help, but what did they mean by dispose of? Were all the expensive canapés just going to be thrown in the trash? They certainly weren't going to be served up again the next day, I was told, and unless I wanted to eat them all myself, I should quit questioning, get to work, and start throwing them all out so we could finally head to the hotel.

And get to work I did. Thank goodness for throwing out all the good food. Like most of us, I was raised in a family where throwing out food was rightly frowned upon. I asked the captain for permission, then set about helping myself to the catering. I sat in the plane's comfortable cabin—a pleasure for which our clients pay around US$4,500 an hour. I was just twenty-two years old, so my metabolism was in great shape. But it was still an ambitious undertaking, and neither of my coworkers was prepared to help out. They had seen all this luxury catering stuff before, and simply weren't interested. What I couldn't eat there and then, I mostly packed in plastic bags and took back with me to the hotel, where I later scarfed down more meatballs until I couldn't for the life of me fit in another mouthful. I hadn't flown any passengers, but there I was, sitting in my hotel room with a belly full of posh catering. I actually felt quite ill from all the food, and the whole episode didn't ultimately strike me as particularly glamorous. Our accommodation was super comfortable, though.

So, there you have it; my first day in a career I had imagined to be so glamorous: a hasty departure, an empty-leg flight, a canceled flight, and a solo assault on the cold buffet. As I said, I had envisaged it differently. At twenty-two, you not only have a strong metabolism; you also have dreams. Over the coming weeks and months, I would learn what my coworkers meant when they said, "you might be sitting at the front in the cockpit, but it's the ones behind you who've really made it." Because, of course, we were simply the staff of the established upper-class and the nouveau riche, of politicians, rock stars, and Hollywood actors who didn't think twice about ordering a plane to spend a weekend in the Mediterranean. We were like spectators of this glamorous lifestyle, doing work, and collecting a plethora of anecdotes along the way. Oh, and meatballs—did I mention those?

CHAPTER

2

A ROLLER-COASTER DESIGNER AND OTHER MAGICAL CAREER ASPIRATIONS

There are some professions where people constantly ask you how you ended up there. Milliners and foot surgeons, for instance. Jobs people tend to hear little about, and which don't necessarily figure in career-orientation programs. When it comes to pilots, however, most people assume you've been dreaming of flying since the age of four. It's one of those classic "dream jobs" little kids have, and many of my coworkers certainly did know what they wanted to do before they were even old enough to read and write.

My first career aspiration was to be a magician. I wanted to amaze people and blow their minds—and I definitely believed many of the tricks being performed at the time were the work of magic. My childhood idol was David Copperfield, who was such a prominent figure in the early '90s that he could afford feature-length shows on Germany's popular RTL television channel—genuine extravaganzas that would see him make entire trains disappear. What most impressed me, however, was a trick in which the master magician flew over the stage. Without any visible aids, he lifted off—just like that—, flew into glass boxes, and carried attractive young women up into the air in his arms. As a young boy in Frankfurt, I even had the opportunity to attend one of his live shows, and it was this particular routine that had a huge impact on me. It would be only a few years until the magician market was claimed by a bespectacled wise guy named Harry Potter. But I would probably have been a Ravenclaw at Hogwarts, or maybe even a Hufflepuff. And that doesn't really involve taking the lead; you're instead stuck in a completely insignificant support role for seven books and eight films. (Let's face it: Flying on a broomstick is not exactly something you'd classify as glamorous, even if it is a Nimbus 2000. Not at a school named after skin growths on a pig butt.) So, my dream of becoming a magician eventually faded from the spotlight.

Back then, I wanted to do something creative in general. I wanted to let my artistic flair run wild. Later, my ideas for a professional career would center more on the talents and preferences that would actually earn me money on the job market. Like nearly everyone in my family, I had always been quite technically gifted and good with my hands. My father renovated and extended our house virtually on his own, while my grandpa was forever tinkering away at cars and motorbikes. Young Patrick was a constant presence, watching over the adults' shoulders and pitching in whenever he could. That was very inspiring for me. I decided I wanted to design roller coasters or cars. Probably airplanes too. After all, someone had to do it, right? I was incessantly drawing little diagrams to immortalize my ideas. This turned out to be an ideal way to combine my technical affinity and my creative streak. But when, a few years later, it came to thinking about how I could turn this hobby into a career, the prospects were pretty dismal and daunting. While I may not have lacked the necessary technical understanding, I was not one for prolonged, theory-based study peppered with numerous stints of work experience. I had always been more of a doer, and I wanted to see and experience the products of my work directly. People who design cars and planes spend a lifetime at the drawing board, often not even being able to savor the fruits of their labor at the end of it all.

I have loved airplanes since early childhood, and had spent many a weekend at the airfields around Frankfurt with my family. We lived in a small town nearby, and there were often air shows or similar events that gave me the opportunity to see daredevil pilots getting into light aircraft and performing bold, gutsy maneuvers. We kids—my brother and I, and all the others—were absolutely mesmerized. Many of us naturally tried to imagine what it would be like to sit in the cockpit and dash through the clouds. I was fascinated but also sad, because I wasn't the one flying the planes.

It was my father who, years later, gave me the idea of training to be a pilot, which had been his dream job. His career ended up taking him in a different direction, and he today works in finance and software. But his simple, probably quite spontaneous suggestion of "Why not get your pilot's license?" resonated with something inside me. I was eighteen, and had almost finished my final school exams, so it was time to start making some concrete plans for the future. My father was pretty much preaching to the converted. It soon became clear that flying would be a good fit for me, and was something I'd like to try. So, I started researching into what pilot training involved, what the prerequisites were, etc. It's worth mentioning here that this "training" was not part of the usual apprenticeship process followed in Germany for "state-certified industrial trades." Instead of completing the standard three-year, part study / part practical apprenticeship, it is sometimes possible—depending on the type of training—to obtain a commercial pilot's license in just eighteen months. (The term "obtain" is itself used rather loosely here, given that it's naturally not something you can just go out and buy. But more on the specific requirements later . . .)

A little crash-landing before takeoff: Finding a flight school

Anyone looking for information on pilot training in 2006 would inevitably find themselves inquiring with Lufthansa, which offered a financed program. This ran for around twenty-four months, and taught you the skills needed to basically fly anything from a hobby plane to an Airbus (with additional training required for the larger aircraft). To qualify for the free training, you had to sit a comprehensive recruitment test. I might only just have started my compulsory civil service at a kindergarten, but what did I have to lose? I registered for the recruitment test, which was to be held at the DLR, the German Aerospace Center, in Hamburg.

I knew very few of the candidates applying for the pilot training would have prior knowledge, but I've always been a determined person who never shied away from extra work or effort, so when I set my mind on something, I manically learn everything I can. I bought software (at the time still on CD-ROM) that had been developed specially for would-be pilots. Memory training, complex mental arithmetic and math, reactivity, personality tests; I crammed like no tomorrow. The recruitment test would be held over two days, and when I finally headed off to Hamburg, I was as well prepared as I could possibly be ...

... only to crash-land on the very first exam. It wasn't for lack of preparation; it was a classic case of exam nerves. I was suddenly distracted by this cheerless room, which was filled with forty candidates who didn't know each other. Unfamiliar faces everywhere, each one of us seemingly hell-bent on prevailing over the others, no matter what. Coupled with this was the stuffy air, the cold fluorescent lighting, and a tense vibe that spread like a virus—and, all of a sudden, I was no longer able to focus on the task at hand. We had to memorize sequences of letters that were shown briefly, and then write them down. I created mnemonics by concocting matching phrases. For example, if the sequence was "HPBTAOFJ," I tried to memorize something like "Harry prays before the altar of Father John." I suspect this only made me more confused, as it wasn't a method I had practiced before. It also had to be done superfast, while the sequences got longer and longer, and I was overcome by nerves. I failed that section so spectacularly that I wasn't able to make up for it in the other sections where I did much better.

It came as little surprise when, soon after, I found out I had flunked the recruitment test. My unexpected exam nerves and those damn letter sequences had brought my dream to an abrupt end. I was totally shattered, and had no idea what to do next. Over the previous few weeks, I had devoted all my energy to the exam preparation. For months, the idea of becoming a pilot had been my motivating force. And now? Nothing.

A friend finally alerted me to the fact that a flying school in Frankfurt—a subsidiary of Lufthansa—was running a private training course. At the time, the school was trading under the name of InterCockpit; today, it is part of the European Flight Academy (EFA), which spans the Lufthansa Group flying schools in Germany, Switzerland, and the USA. The whole thing had a similar structure to the training I had unsuccessfully applied for, except that it would be held in different places—and trainees would not receive any funding; they had to finance everything themselves. The total costs amounted to more than 70,000 euros (about US$80,000). I weighed up my options. I asked people who were currently undertaking the training to find out if it would be my thing too. (Unfortunately, there was no social media at the time, and consequently no Instagram account of a young pilot providing detailed work updates for his followers . . .)

The information I managed to glean from my mini interviews left me with a really positive feeling. While it was a full-time course, there was a chance I might even be able to do some part-time work on the side. Plus, I would be able to live at home—at least for the units held in Frankfurt—and thus save a lot of money. In any case, I was in no doubt I really wanted to be a pilot. The failed exam hadn't put me off at all. I knew I had just let the whole occasion get to me.

Nevertheless—and this seemed to be the biggest problem of all—I was still far from being able to scratch up the necessary money. My parents were pretty pragmatic about it: If I had gone to college, I would not have been able to obtain any education grants, and would instead have been dependent on their financial support. A six-year (or more) course would have cost them a considerable sum, which would probably have ended up similar to the costs for pilot training. So why not invest the money in this course? We weren't a wealthy family—70,000 euros was a really large amount for my parents. At the same time, I realize other families simply wouldn't have been able to afford it at all. So, I was ultimately in a pretty privileged position, and I am grateful for that. It enabled me to get an early start in an established training course for a career that would provide me with a relatively secure future.

I submitted my application, and once again began preparing for the qualification test that was, of course, also required here. It particularly tested my knowledge of math, physics, and English. This time it went well; I passed the tests without any problem. (For purely financial reasons, the flying school was no doubt keen for the courses to be well attended; that said, nothing was handed to us on a platter.) I also had to undergo a medical check—a "Class 1 medical"— in Stuttgart with a specialist physician. But, as was to be expected for an athletic young man, there were no medical grounds preventing me from following my intended career path. InterCockpit also gave me the all-clear soon after. The fact I was able to provide proof of having been accepted into a training course in turn meant I was allowed to finish my compulsory civil service earlier than planned. Otherwise the final weeks at the kindergarten would have clashed with the start of my training, and I would have had to wait an entire year for the next course. So, after the initial failure to launch, everything was finally going swimmingly for me.

Incidentally, I still, to this day, have a fractious relationship with Hamburg, where I so spectacularly failed my first exam. Yes, I know it wasn't the wildly popular Hanseatic city that had conspired against me that day. It's not Hamburg's fault that I was totally incapable of memorizing a sequence of letters while under stress in a large, stuffy room. So, I'd like to take this opportunity to give a particularly big shout-out to all my readers from Hamburg—it's nothing against you, guys. But I don't think Hamburg and I will be besties any time soon . . .

From ATC to WTF?!:
Some initial theory and pilot jargon

It was in April 2008, about a month before my twentieth birthday, that I began my training that would eventually secure me a "frozen ATPL." "ATPL" stands for "Airline Transport Pilot License," and it would be "frozen," because the license only becomes a fully valid ATPL once you've recorded enough hours of flying. Fifteen hundred, to be precise. So, it was going to take a while. Until then, the "frozen" ATPL would be my CPL (Commercial Pilot License). (I know qualified pilots who never totally understood the difference between "frozen ATPL," "CPL," and "ATPL." It's complicated.)

Of the twenty-one trainees (only one of whom was female), I was the second youngest. I had already managed to find my first friend in Fabian, whom I had met during the medical check in Stuttgart. But I was still very nervous. To feel anything else would probably have been foolish anyway; after all, I was starting a completely new stage of life. And though I initially continued to live with my parents, those first few days at InterCockpit were like my first steps into adulthood. I'm sure we all remember our first day of an apprenticeship or college. It's that mix of confidence and fear, of grand plans and self-doubt, that engraves such days in our memory.

First there was the compulsory orientation, during which our fellow trainees, the teaching staff, and the academy itself were introduced to us. We were then provided with our course materials: About ten thick, bulging folders that, collectively, looked like an almost insurmountable pile of work. While I of course wouldn't let myself be discouraged by this, I also made sure I was under no illusions: The next eighteen months were going to require real, uncompromising dedication. Airy-fairy attitudes weren't going to get any of us anywhere. We were each also given a typical, black pilot's case to help us lug the folders to class each day. (At the time I was really proud of it, but today it lies unused in my basement. Traveling as much as I do, I tend to steer clear of any luggage item that doesn't have four wheels on the bottom and a handle on top.)

In a number of disciplines, learning by doing quickly leads to demonstrable success. For example, many people get their first taste of driving a car in an empty parking lot, as friends or parents explain to them how the brakes, accelerator, and clutch work. Then they try it all out themselves to see how they go. For obvious reasons, that would be a very bad idea in a plane. Pilot training, of course, doesn't start with you getting straight into the cockpit to do a few trial laps. (Though, I must admit, it's a nice idea. In general, with training that costs as much as this does, it would be good to somehow be able to get an idea of it to see if you've chosen the right career. If any of the fine people at the EFA are listening: Trainees should at least be given a few free hours in the flight simulator.)

So, we first had two months of theory ahead of us, teaching us what we needed to know to get a PPL or Private Pilot License. We also learned the necessary terms (and functions) for the radiotelephone operator license, without which the dream of getting your pilot license can never come true. The General Radiotelephone Operator License (GROL) enables private and commercial pilots to communicate with air traffic control, ATC for short. This required the aforementioned English skills. Radio contacts in German are permitted for flights within German airspace, but on international flights, all communication must be in English. It's the only way to guarantee that the cockpit and control tower can successfully communicate with one another in the event of an emergency. So, to recap: The GROL enables you to communicate with ATC (which is part of the DFS, Deutsche Flugsicherung, the company in charge of air traffic control in Germany) for both the ATPL and the PPL. I was gradually starting to see why we had been tortured with those letter sequences in Hamburg; sometimes you'd see them and just think "WTF??" Fortunately, I was now much better at memorizing all the abbreviations.

After two months of theory, we were finally able to start the first practical component of the training in June. We would actually be flying. First in a simulator, so on the ground, but then in a real plane. There's the "10,000-hours rule," which is, ultimately, just another way of saying "practice makes perfect." To become a master in any discipline, you need to practice, practice, practice for 10,000 long hours. The more often you perform certain actions, the more ingrained they become, until, at some point, you can do them in your sleep, as it were. While 10,000 hours of practice would, of course, have well exceeded the scope of the training, what we had been doing so far had indeed been simply practicing, practicing, practicing. This gradually gave rise to a feeling of unease, because we all knew it would soon be time to put our learning to the test.

Have fun . . . and "happy landings": My first flight

To do this, all of us headed to Zadar, a small town in Croatia, a little over 620 miles from Frankfurt, in June for ten weeks. There were several reasons why this training unit was held in a different country. The two most important of these for us were: The lower costs in Croatia helped bring down the super-high training expenses. Zadar also had better flying weather for us "pedestrians"—the aviation term for people with no flying experience.

We had to organize our travel arrangements and accommodation ourselves. For the people of Zadar, the regular presence of German trainee pilots had ceased to be a novelty. Most of us stayed in accommodation run by a woman whose primary source of income came from aspiring pilots like us. Fabian and I rented a small apartment from her. It essentially had everything we needed, and was right by the picturesque coast—because Zadar is located on a narrow headland on the Adriatic Sea; the Dalmatian Coast, to be precise. The city, which today has a population of around 75,000, looks back on a turbulent history—it has been ruled by the likes of the Romans, the Byzantines, the Franconians, the Venetians, and the Austro-Hungarians, among others. The stunning old town is situated right on the water, where we would spend the evenings watching spectacular sunsets. Things could definitely have been worse.

In actual fact, the whole of Croatia is an absolutely amazing sight when seen from the cockpit. Dozens of small, even tiny, islands—sixty-six of them inhabited—rise up out of the Adriatic's turquoise waters. The coast stretches for 1,120 miles, flanked by the Biokovo Mountains. In short: a genuine paradise.

This was where we would take to the skies for the first time. We were all excited, sure. Many of us were scared too. Personally, I was worried less about the flying and more about whether I had actually made the right decision to undertake this training. Everything had gone well so far, but things were getting even more real now with the first solo flights. That can make you a little nervous—after all, it was my professional future, not to mention a shedload of money.

For some, even the sight of the DA20 Katana was enough to cause jitters. The two-seater made by Austrian company Diamond Aircraft ended up being nicknamed "the yogurt cup," because it was made almost entirely of plastic. The plane itself only weighed 1,170 pounds, and, with a full fuel load, would barely have had enough range to return to Frankfurt. The first time I saw it on the ground, I instinctively exclaimed, "That thing flies?" I felt it totally appropriate to have a little healthy skepticism. The cockpit was so cramped I felt as if I was in a coffin. The whole thing was somehow unsettling, and I was relieved to learn that we would be doing our first few laps in the air under the watchful eye of Wolle, our flying instructor. Wolle was an unshakable optimist, always willing to intervene if anything threatened to go awry. "At first, the trainees want to kill you," he often joked, primarily as a way of explaining to us that it was also in his interest to teach us as well as possible. After all, he was the one who had to keep getting into the plane with us.

A few days later, it was time: Each of us would be doing a solo flight. Wolle would stay on the ground and provide instructions and information by radio. But apart from that, we were on our own. My fear of taking to the skies in this flying plastic coffin suddenly also got a lot more real. I went through every conceivable horror scenario in my head. Because anyone who's well prepared will also be aware of all the things that can potentially happen.

"Just do what you normally do—have fun and 'happy landings'!" were Wolle's short-and-sweet words to me as he sent me on my way. Do what I normally do? This was my first flight. Have fun? My heart was beating out of my damn chest. Overall, there was a strange disparity between the pointedly casual way our flying instructor went about the whole matter— what else could he do?—and the automatic, resistant human instinct to ask, through chattering teeth: "Do you really think it's a good idea to get into this tin can and fly a few laps 1,000 feet above ground?" These doubts are purely self-preservationist, and refuse to be swayed by the fact that you understand the physics of aeronautics. I wasn't actually putting myself in a dangerous situation. I had the preflight inspection, which involves checking the oil levels and technical functionality of all equipment, down pat. I was familiar with all the other procedures, too. I knew what I had to do. But when you squeeze yourself into that tiny cockpit on your own for the first time, there's always that niggling thought of "what if...?"

Another "tip" commonly given by Wolle was also floating around in my brain: "Make sure you hit the runway." It was a pragmatic approach with a serious basis. Much of the ground here had been a minefield during the Yugoslav Wars, and you never knew how many unexploded bombs were still under the soil. The runway was safe, but if you missed it, there was definitely a chance of barely hitting the ground before being sent straight back up into the air by an exploding mine. My landings in the flight simulator had been less than impressive. But there was no turning back now. With a queasy feeling in my stomach, I walked over to the plane. In any case, I looked the part: In my gray pilot overalls and aviators, it was like shades of Maverick, Tom Cruise's character in the classic movie *Top Gun*.

After the initial check of the plane's exterior, I climbed into the cockpit. Deep breath. Engage the parking brake: Check. Close and lock the bubble canopy: Check. Deep breath. Then put on seatbelt and check again. Deep breath. Was I really ready? And if not, what other choice did I have right now? Deep breath! I went through the second checklist, the one for the cockpit equipment. Check, check, check ... and another deep breath. The seat next to me was vacant. Instructor Wolle was standing some distance away outside, confident and attentive, but of course not remotely as nervous as me. I, on the other hand ... well ... deep breath!

Each of us was to do several "touch-and-go traffic patterns," in which the pilot follows the airport's set traffic pattern. Every airport has one, with a set flight path and cruising altitude. The circuits are generally counterclockwise, so turning to the left. The pilot starts up the plane and makes it airborne. Soon after takeoff, at an altitude of around 500 feet, he makes a sharp, 90-degree left turn into what is known as the crosswind leg. Another 500 feet up, he stops the ascent at 1,000 feet, makes another 90-degree turn to the left, and flies parallel to the runway in the downwind leg. Then he starts to prepare his approach. Having engaged the engine throttle and flaps, it's another left turn into the crosswind leg, and, then, after one last left turn, into the short final approach for the plane to briefly touch down on the runway ("Hit the runway," don't forget!), before taking off again for another few laps.

To those who think this is all an overly complicated way of simply saying, "flying around in circles for a while," I would retort with an emphatic "Yes, but!" While route length and steering are kept very simple, the traffic patterns are quite a challenging maneuver, particularly for beginners, as you need to do a lot of things all at once. In addition to the takeoffs and landings, and the actual flying, I had to make radio calls, read checklists, keep an eye on the air traffic around me, have a view of the runway at all times while navigating, and be aware of any obstacles. Everything had to happen simultaneously or in very quick succession.

In any case, the weather was on my side. Just light winds, which would make landing easier. I got my radio clearance for takeoff, without which I wouldn't be allowed to start up the plane's rather complex piston engine. For days I had been vividly imagining mortifying scenarios in which I wasn't even able to get the thing running. Fortunately, none of these happened. On receiving the okay, I shouted the standard "CLEAR PROP!" through the little porthole, so that anyone still nearby would know I was about to get going and that they needed to hotfoot it away from the plane. I then turned the key in the ignition system—incidentally, a surprisingly small, thin piece of metal, not much different from a locker key. Next, I flicked the ignition switch, and heard the engine spring to life. First shot. Yeah, baby! I grabbed the controls and it was go time. I taxied to runway 32, as instructed. This required interrupting the regular road traffic between the airport's two runways, so that I could head past the cars and move from one runway to the other. It must have looked pretty funny, because the windscreens of the cars I taxied past were almost at the same level as mine. I also had to zigzag around the numerous craters of varying depths that pockmarked the asphalt—another product of the Yugoslav Wars.

"Cleared for takeoff, Runway 32," came the final radio message. There was no turning back now. I switched on the fuel pump and taxi light, set the transponder and heading indicator, adjusted the artificial horizon, and did another check—trust, but verify!—to make sure the short final approach behind me was clear. I then started taxiing the DA20 Katana, turned it up to full power—and took off. I was airborne. On my own. No flying instructor next to me controlling the plane. As expected, I had little time to think. Everything had to be done as automatically as possible—ascent, turn, ascent, turn, and, having reached cruising altitude, I was already on the downwind leg. I let out a loud cry of joy.

But I didn't have time to enjoy the feeling. I had to do two more turns to start the descent again, before briefly touching down and starting the next lap. Things got tricky after the second lap. The wind changed direction, prompting the air traffic controller on the ground to instruct me to change course. As there were a couple of us in the air at the time, I was now on a collision course with another trainee. No instructions came from the air traffic controller, so I queried it, and was told to follow a different course. All I can say is, you really need to keep your eyes open when in the air.

I spent a whole thirty minutes up there doing my laps. But it felt much shorter. Time literally seemed to fly during those first few laps. Then it was time for the final descent. I sat up, alert, taxied to a stop, and parked the plane. I switched off everything that needed to be switched off, and turned the key again to kill the engine. As I climbed out of the tiny cockpit and back onto solid ground, my whole body felt like it had been working out for hours. Only now did I notice the stress and tension I had been under during the flight. It all just fell like weights off my shoulders, leaving behind nothing but relief. I had done it. My first solo flight. I was bursting with pride and joy. Any doubts I had had about whether I had chosen the right training were dispelled. Instead, I could hardly wait to get back in the air.

I had flown as a passenger countless times. The first time was in 1990, when I was not even two, for a vacation in Mallorca with my parents and grandparents. (My younger brother hadn't yet been born.) Four weeks prior, we had visited Frankfurt airport with relatives from East Germany. They had wanted to do the outing now that they were finally able to travel to the West. Nobody had asked little Patrick, but, in any case, I couldn't have dreamed of a better destination. It was definitely much more exciting than grandpa's motorbike at home. Watching the planes take off and land was such a buzz. I knew we would soon be flying in one of them ourselves. I suspect I didn't think of much else over the weeks that followed. Incidentally, my father was just as excited as I was, but not entirely without fear. He actually had his will drawn up before we left. We departed on my grandma's 50th birthday, which the adults toasted with sparkling wine above the clouds. I assume that calmed my father's nerves a little.

During the flight, I was attended to by a stewardess who had obviously taken a shine to me. To this day, I always make sure I'm a good, attentive, and helpful coworker to the cabin crew—that's just basic decency—, though I like to think that lovely lady had something to do with it too.

My grandpa remembers me being bright as a button on the plane, taking a keen interest in everything. As he shares my passion for planes, he was definitely the one most able out of all the adults to understand my enthusiasm. Before being called up for military service in 1941, his father had worked at the Junkers factories—Junkers being the company that made the legendary Ju 52 light aircraft, which went down in aviation history as "Aunt Ju." He had left a few photographs from this time for his son, and they continue to hang in my grandpa's house to this day. Something about those photos really grabbed me. One photo in particular; the one showing my great-grandpa standing in front of Aunt Ju. This aircraft had originally been designed as a cargo plane, but in World War II, the old aunt was given a very grim role, which included the task of bombing Warsaw.

I also spent many vacations in Portugal, where one of my uncles came from. In 1996, at the age of eight, I went on my first intercontinental flight—to America, with my paternal grandma. So, I was quite a jetsetter right from a young age. But I particularly remember my first flight in one of the small, single-engine planes I so loved to watch at our local sport airfields. My grandparents had taken me and my little brother to an air show in Obernhain, not long after my America trip. These events were always a bit like funfairs, with snack stalls and raffles. I actually won one of those raffles, and the prize was a flight in a light airplane. My grandpa bought a second ticket so that he could accompany me. We spent twenty minutes flying through the air. Awestruck and with heart racing, I watched the pilot's every move—I had never been so close to the action before. To top it all off, initially we weren't given clearance to land, because another plane was "blocking" our approach; old Aunt Ju got her clearance to land before us, which meant we ended up spending nearly three quarters of an hour in the air. The pilot even allowed my grandpa to take over the control stick, which had a huge impact on me. He really only performed a few, relatively easy functions following the pilot's instructions; but to me, it signaled that my grandpa could also fly a plane! I always knew he was the best.

The plane is refueled, but not the pilot: Flying lessons in Zadar

The following training weeks in Zadar saw us keep practicing VFR (visual flight rules) flights. We learned different manual maneuvers to ensure the number one rule of aviation became fully ingrained in us: Aviate, navigate, communicate! In that order. Most important of all is to concentrate on the flight processes at all times, to ensure the plane stays up in the air. Navigating ensures the plane stays in safe zones, far enough away from any obstacles. It also includes setting and keeping the plane on course, and landing. Point number three is about communicating with the air traffic controllers. This is, of course, also a vitally important part of standard procedures, though in cases of doubt, pilots must equally be able to function when unable to communicate with those on the ground for any reason.

We also practiced stalls, which are done by angling the wing to cause an almost total loss of dynamic lift. We practiced "steep turns," which tilted the plane more than thirty degrees, and "slow flights," which are particularly challenging, because the plane reacts differently to control commands than it would in normal or high-speed flights.

Having been familiarized with the various procedures and the plane itself, as well as flight trajectories and radio communication, it was finally time for our first cross-country flights.

These, too, would be VFR flights that we would navigate ourselves, except they wouldn't be preset, closely marked out laps; they would be A-to-B routes between two different airports—a starting point and a landing point. For some of these flights, we would use a Diamond DA40, a four-seater light aircraft with a four-cylinder piston engine. You sit at the front with the instructor, and another trainee could sit behind you. Positions are then usually swapped for the return flight. One afternoon, we flew to a small airport in Slovenia. Upon landing, we were met by a little motorbike, which guided us to our parking position. The plane was refueled before flying back. While this was happening, the engineer offered us a sample of his homebrewed booze. There is simply no instance in which this kind of "simultaneous plane and pilot refuel" wouldn't be utterly negligent and inappropriate. Nevertheless, the guy was quite a character himself, and we had a lot of fun with him.

The training weeks were intense and thrilling. We were always experiencing something new, focused fully on processing and addressing the myriad things that cropped up while flying. There was also time for a few "overland" excursions. I particularly remember Krka National Park, with its spectacular waterfalls. But apart from that, every spare minute was spent learning. In the evening, Fabian and I often performed "chair flying" for each other. It's a method that has been used for decades (and continues to be used today) to internalize the actions and flows learned in training. As the name suggests, you sit on a chair, as if in a cockpit, pretending to reach for the steering wheel, controls, etc. It's a particularly good way to prepare for flying aircraft you're not yet familiar with. "Don't forget!" went the motto, "You need to fly the plane; the plane doesn't fly you."

Glide landings in the event of engine failure were one of the things we had practiced in the simulator. The chances of this actually succeeding are of course higher when you're at a higher cruising altitude and closer to the runway. It's a rather delicate maneuver in general, and not something you'd ideally want to be trying out in a real emergency. But I wasn't spared the experience. On a solo cross-country flight, I noticed, on approach to Pula airport, that there were issues with my plane's engine. I couldn't work out what exactly was wrong, but something was definitely up. So I stayed near the airport to ensure I would be able to go into a glide if the propeller failed. It's definitely not a situation you want to be in as an inexperienced trainee pilot, but I went by the book and safely landed the plane, which was then taken away to the workshop. I never found out what the actual problem was, but I noticed it was out of action for several days thereafter. The repairs must have been quite extensive—and, to this day, I take that as a clear sign that I had had a lucky escape.

It's always wise to study: The first exams

After ten weeks of VFR flying in Zadar, we returned to Frankfurt for the next theory component of the course. It would now be more than eight months before we'd be back in a cockpit. It was a painful prospect for most of us, because we'd now caught the flying bug. Flying is addictive. But we still had a lot to learn. This in-depth second phase of theory would be teaching us everything we needed to know for our commercial pilot license (reminder: the "frozen" ATPL). The subsequent ATPL exam would mark the end of this part of the course, and thus also constitute the theory component of the exam.

Based on everything we had heard from the year groups above us, the LBA, Germany's civil aviation authority that ran the exam, didn't bother putting together new papers every year. It was mostly multiple-choice questions that you could properly prepare for, using the Peters software, for example. Ultimately—so it seemed—we wouldn't need to do anything more than intensively learn the test questions and corresponding answers. I found that dumb right from the outset. I had come to learn something, and felt it was prudent to know what I had to do in my future profession. I didn't want to negligently bluff my way through the exams by simply ticking boxes in certain orders in response to questions. So I once again threw myself into study. I studied like a man possessed. I wanted to understand the concepts.

Many others evidently took the easier option, simply learning questions and answers by heart. This became apparent when the actual exams rolled around: For the first time in many years, the LBA had decided to adjust the exam process. Twelve exams in twelve subjects—general navigation, meteorology, radio navigation, the principles of flight (my personal favorite), air traffic laws, powerplant, instruments and electronics, flight planning, operational procedures, performance, and weight and balance—took place over a period of three days.

Being the lowest year group, we were asked lots of open questions that required proving you had actually understood what you had learned, and were able to apply this flexibly. Those of us who had studied the course material in detail—like me—now had a clear advantage. But we were in the minority: Of the twenty pupils, a whopping fifteen had to re-sit the exams. This time, unlike my Hamburg experience, I was mega-pleased with my results; I scored at least 87 percent in every subject. In two thirds of them, I actually scored above 95 percent. I really couldn't have done much better. Overall, I had passed with an average of 94 percent—well above the required pass mark of 75 percent. What was particularly pleasing—for me, at least—was that I topped the class

The first tragedy of my young flying career

In addition to the many hours of study, that summer was also marred by a very dramatic event for us trainee pilots. In early August, we heard that a fellow trainee—an Italian guy just nineteen years of age—had crashed in Croatia with a 35-year-old instructor. The pair had taken off in Zadar, suffered a stall just 25 miles into the flight, and crashed into the sea. According to the accident report, the instructor had assessed the risk incorrectly, and consequently intervened too late. The accident occurred on August 1, 2008. The wreck, containing the two bodies, wasn't recovered for another two days; it was lying on the sea floor, at a depth of 223 feet. Some of us were at Kira's (the only female trainee in our course) birthday party when we heard the news. It really shook us.

There was no deeper meaning to be drawn from a tragedy like this; we all knew there was always a risk of crashing in aviation, even though the statistics show this happens very rarely. Going purely by the numbers, airplanes are the safest mode of transport. But that doesn't change the fact that, when an accident does occur, it is much more likely to kill those involved compared to an accident in another mode of transport. The tragedy demonstrated this to us trainee pilots in dramatic fashion very early on in our training. And as is sometimes also the case in these sorts of accidents, someone else had a miraculous escape: The second trainee, who had actually been meant to accompany the cross-country flight, had slept in that morning and hadn't gotten to the airport on time, so the other two flew without him.

It may sound corny and clichéd, but the accident really opened my eyes to how quickly something can happen to us. We put ourselves in any number of precarious situations on a daily basis, which is why it is all the more important to live life to the full. Be brave without being careless. Be optimistic without being naive. And, no matter whether you're walking on air or flying into a rage, pay attention as you land.

A rocket launch in a pensioner paradise: My IFR flight training in Florida

After several long months of theory, it was back to beautiful Zadar in May 2009 for more practical flight training. But shortly before leaving, we received news that, for logistical reasons, lodging there was not going to be possible, and a new training location thus had to be found. This was sad news for us, as we had all fallen a little in love with that town. But our disappointment didn't last long, because we soon found out where we would be going instead: Vero Beach, Florida, on the southeastern coast of the USA. As I was one of the few who had passed the exams first shot, I was also one of the first to be allowed to fly on a Lufthansa A340-300 from Dusseldorf to Miami. From there, it was another two-and-a-half-hour drive to Vero Beach.

Vero Beach airport had its own FlightSafety campus on site (FlightSafety being the name of the American flying school), where we were all housed in apartments, with two or more of us sharing each apartment. These were simple, no-frills, two-story buildings, though we did have a small, common swimming pool. Nearby were stunning beaches that we went to in what little free time we had. Apart from that, there was not much else to see or do in Florida, which is, after all, America's pensioner paradise—the sidewalks were rolled up at 1 a.m. This did, however, make it easier for us to concentrate on our flying training without any distractions. Trainee pilots from all over the world came together here, and FlightSafety had ninety planes available for lessons, so we never ran short.

Having learned VFR flying in Zadar, the curriculum now shifted to instrument flying, which involves following instrument flight rules (IFR), and almost always coordinating with air traffic control. The difference between VFR and IFR is actually pretty self-explanatory: VFR rely on two healthy eyes and correct decision-making; IFR are about steering the plane largely without any external visual reference points, depending instead on navigation instruments and the flight-monitoring systems in the cockpit. Air traffic controllers on the ground provide additional assistance during takeoff and landing in the form of clearances for specified departure routes and maximum altitudes. In standard flight operations, IFR are common practice, whereas VFR are only used in exceptional cases. These cases also include takeoff and—around 95 percent of the time—landing, which are flown according to VFR. (That's also why, in bad weather, you sometimes have to spend hours waiting onboard before you finally take off. We don't do that to annoy you. I promise.)

When we arrived in Vero Beach in early May, we were met with high-summer temperatures. Florida provided the perfect conditions for our flight training. There are several small airports close to Vero Beach, making it a particularly great place to practice traffic patterns, approaches, and holding patterns. The weather and the vast, flat landscapes are ideal for any pilot—but especially for trainees. While spring and summer do bring a lot of storms, these are usually just isolated weather phenomena that are easily visible from afar, and which you can fly around—and this, too, must of course be practiced.

This time, our training plane was a Piper Arrow, a four-seater with a piston engine. We all had to do twenty-two flight missions, each around four hours long. Half of this time would be spent flying ourselves, and the other half sitting in the observer watching a fellow trainee fly. To simulate realistic conditions for IFR flights, we wore large glasses when at the wheel, to restrict the view out the window. We usually flew from Vero Beach to one of the surrounding airports, including, for the first time, larger airports with high traffic volumes—something I found particularly exciting. It was pretty awesome to fly among the large passenger jets.

These were also exciting and challenging weeks for me in other ways. I had to get used to a new type of aircraft and new flight procedures, which went well overall. What I found challenging was communicating with the air traffic controllers, who spoke in such broad American slang that I had trouble understanding them. But as pilots can't choose their air traffic controllers any more than air traffic controllers can choose their pilots, it's good to get an ear for all kinds of dialects. Two flights from my time in Florida have particularly stuck with me: One time, I was planning and operating a flight from Vero Beach to Miami Executive Airport, which is very frequently used by private jets. Once there, we parked next to a Gulfstream jet—an ultra-luxurious business jet—right outside an equally swanky terminal for private planes. The terminal provided excellent service for both crew and passengers: There was a pool table, a mini library, and even a cinema. I mentioned at the start that I am one of those people who have a thing for aesthetically pleasing glamour, so I was in my element here. The private jet and this terminal really were a feast for the eyes. To top it off even further, our return flight went eastward over the stunningly beautiful coastal city of Miami Beach. Fortunately, we had been given the necessary clearance by air traffic control. The huge volumes of traffic at Miami International Airport meant that in itself was a rarity. We then flew past the airport at a lower cruising altitude, before heading toward Miami Beach—and the view was simply spectacular. Even my instructor was impressed: "It's so amazing, you have to see it," he said, and allowed me to take off my blinkers.

My flight to the Space Coast Regional Airport in Titusville, Florida, was another highlight. This coastal airport is located near the legendary Cape Canaveral, the section of coast whose southern tip is home to the United States' most important space mission launch centers: NASA's Kennedy Space Center for all human space flights, and the Cape Canaveral Air Force Station, where uncrewed rocket launches are held. My lesson that day was focusing on go-arounds and the relevant reaction patterns in the cockpit. (Yes, even go-arounds need to be practiced; it's about knowing what you need to do if an approach needs to be aborted for safety reasons. In a nutshell: The plane needs to ascend again, so it can "go around" and reattempt the landing.) We were approaching the airport when we received an unexpected radio request: In the airspace above the Cape Canaveral launch pad (which is out-of-bounds for pilots) was an unknown aircraft with which the control tower was unable to establish radio contact. We were asked if we could approach the plane and try and make out its aircraft registration number. We, of course, accepted the request, for it meant we had official permission to enter the off-limits airspace. This was all just a few days before a space shuttle launch, and we could see the space shuttle itself on the launch pad from the cockpit window. A once-in-a-lifetime opportunity, and an awesome, unforgettable moment for me. Unfortunately, however, we weren't able to see the other aircraft's registration number.

Cape Canaveral was a real highlight of our Florida stay in general. During our free time, we visited the NASA Museum, with its amazing exhibition. It's an absolute must for any aerospace enthusiast. I was also super fortunate to be able to watch the space shuttle launch from one of the surrounding beaches. We were many miles away, but the noise that accompanied the spectacle was so loud it was enough to give me goose bumps. Other leisure activities I can recommend to anyone visiting Florida are a cruise along Ocean Drive (ideally do it in style by renting a convertible), and a ride on the cool roller coasters at the Busch Gardens theme park. With its stunning beaches, Miami Beach is a must-see city, while Orlando, with its famous Walt Disney Resort, is the undisputed theme-park capital of the world. Those wanting to turn up the glam factor in their life will also enjoy checking out the giant premium-brand outlet mall here.

Ten tips for aspiring pilots

All this talk of picturesque landscapes, exciting special assignments above space mission launch centers, and folders packed full of learning material will no doubt have made at least some of you out there want to apply for flying school training. More than ten years since I first started out, I can only say that I have not regretted my decision. I love my job.

The coronavirus pandemic has left many industries worldwide on shaky ground. An almost unimaginable number of travel bans, border closures, and similar restrictions have caused havoc in the airline industry. But we will always need new pilots. To give you a few general hints and tips on what to bear in mind when starting your training, I've put together my top 10 list of the things to know about becoming a pilot.

First, it's worth reiterating that there are different types of licenses: There's the PPL (Private Pilot License) for—as the name suggests—private individuals wanting to fly light aircraft for noncommercial purposes. Then there's the CPL (or CPL-A, for Commercial Pilot License Airplane), which entitles holders to fly as a First Office (FO) for commercial airlines. Finally, there's the ATPL (Aircraft Transport Pilot License), which CPL-holders can obtain by sitting an additional theory exam and demonstrating at least 1,500 hours of flying. If you've completed the theory component without amassing the necessary number of flying hours, your license will show as "ATPL Theory Credit," resulting in the "frozen ATPL" I mentioned earlier on. To eventually become a captain for commercial airlines, you need a fully valid ATPL. So that's the dry, formal stuff—now for a lighter approach:

1. It's important to be in good physical shape. The specific requirements for passing the Class 1 medical are readily available online. Some doctors actually specialize in these screening tests as aviation medical examiners. These medicals will continue to be routinely conducted throughout your flying career, so it's advisable to avoid being a couch potato in general. Athleticism and a fit, healthy body are important prerequisites.

2. You will need to enjoy math and physics. You don't need to be a straight-A student, but you should at least have a decent grasp of them. To have a good spatial awareness is mandatory. The specific requirements aren't always the same for every flying school and airline, so research online to find out what the criteria are.

3. Find a flying school whose offering fits your needs. Not all courses have the same structure, and location and cost are also factors that each person needs to assess for themselves. In addition to the schools' online presentations, you can also take advantage of on-site visits (open days), and talk to trainees directly.

4. Try to arrange a short test flight with an instructor to find out whether aviation is the right career path for you.

Nearly everyone wanting to be a pilot will have flown as a passenger at some point, but things look different from the cockpit—and you'll then probably also understand what Leonardo da Vinci meant when he wrote "Once you have tasted flight, you will forever walk the earth with your eyes turned skyward. For there you have been, and there you will always long to return." It's my favorite quote ever.

5. From a financial perspective, it's advisable to go through airline training programs, which usually cover the training costs and offer you a pilot job at the end. Part of the training costs is repaid to the company through your salary. They don't eat up all your salary, of course, and the whole thing is done in manageable installments.

6. Those who, like me, wish to or are forced to go through one of the many private schools around should once again be reminded of the high costs involved. In my case, it was the equivalent of about US$80,000, but they can be anywhere from US$56,000 to US$170,000 (!), depending on the school. In addition, this doesn't even cover expenses for living, eating, leisure, etc. The curriculum is so densely packed, and the training so time-intensive, that there's very little opportunity to fit in a part-time job.

7. Modular training is another possible solution for those who can only afford the costs little by little. The course is

then taken in individual modules, section by section, and so can be stretched out over a longer period of time. Many people even take out a special loan to fulfill their dream of getting their pilot license. So, it's all the more important to be totally sure that this is the right career for you. Once you've got your license, you'll still need to actually find a job, and if things don't go as planned, you'll be left with a bunch of debts and no income.

8. Another reminder here that a pilot license is not, at least in Germany, classified as a state-certified apprenticeship. For example, if a pilot doesn't pass a medical, he or she is not allowed to fly. So it's a good idea to have an alternative or Plan B. Many people first complete a regular vocational training course or university studies before going for their pilot license.

9. I also recommend attending trade fairs where various airlines and training providers are exhibiting. This gives you a chance to ask questions, and also make some initial contacts. In aviation, like many industries, it never does any harm to use a few connections.

10. As you can see from this list, lists are awesome. Go ahead and make your own Pros and Cons list. If, for example, having a fixed location is important to you, you should be aware that pilots are expected to be very flexible. A job change often involves moving to another city or even

another country, and those who value set hours and an after-work beer on the couch should perhaps focus more on an office job instead

Back to Zadar: The third and final practical phase

The second practical phase was quickly followed by the third and final one—this time, back in Zadar, Croatia. Our training was nearly done, and we were now expected to be able to actively recall, at any time, all the knowledge—both theory-based and practical—we had acquired over the last eighteen months. The fact that we would now be flying a twin-engine plane, a Piper PA-44, meant we really had to buckle down. While this was still a light airplane, the two engines made its controls much more complex. It was also an expensive exercise compared to flying a single-engine plane, which is why we only had a short time to familiarize ourselves with the PA-44 and its features. All of these flights were IFR flights.

I finally had my last check flight—basically a practical test—with an examiner from the German aviation authority on August 31, 2009. The guy had actually flown in specially from Germany on a small prop plane, which was pretty extravagant in itself. Considering his travel expenses were part of our exam fees, it seemed a bit presumptuous. It cost over US$1,000, thank you very much; a commercial flight would have been much cheaper.

I had planned my own flight route based on the exam requirements. It went from Zadar to Pula and back, via Lošinj. A total flying time of more than two and a half hours. All my cockpit skills would be put to the test, and I also had to demonstrate that I was fully familiar with the EU-OPS. These EU regulations establish the minimum safety standards for commercial aviation, and provide information on recommended actions, for everything from all-weather operation to time-recording. The examiner would not intervene or assist unless absolutely necessary, and would instead act like a curious passenger, asking questions about any random aspect of aviation. We wouldn't be meeting him until the test itself. There would be no second trainee in the plane this time either; we were all on our own. Needless to say, I was insanely nervous.

I had chosen an airport with a relatively short runway, meaning the asphalt had nearly run out by the time I got the plane airborne. I don't remember much about the flight itself, but my many, many hours of study paid off: I handled all the procedures confidently, and had no brain fades. Having safely landed the plane back in Zadar, the examiner announced I had passed, and I celebrated this news by jumping straight into the Adriatic—in full pilot gear.

My goal had been to not only meet the requirements, but to master them. It had been eighteen extremely challenging months, and never in my life had I needed to buckle down so intensely. I now felt that mix of pride and relief that comes over you when a stress is suddenly lifted off your shoulders.

Trial session in the simulator

The course finished with MCC (Multi Crew Coordination) training, which took place back in Frankfurt after the third practical phase. It only went for a few days, and was designed to give us a feel of what it's like to work with a flight crew—after all, we had so far only flown as "lone wolves." Anyone wanting to fly a commercial airline needs to have completed the MCC training, because being a professional pilot also means recognizing that you are part of a team. While we were now able to fly a plane, any job would see us subordinate to the captain, who is the one calling the shots in the cockpit. Stewards and stewardesses are also part of the crew. Because there's a lot of responsibility on everyone, we all need to know who is in charge of what, and which rules apply in each case. This is precisely what was demonstrated to us in simulated flight scenarios during the MCCT. We were allowed to choose whether we wanted to complete the course in a Boeing B737 simulator or an Airbus A320 simulator. I opted for the Airbus.

If you've never really given much thought to flight simulators before, you probably have a pretty abstract idea of them. They're not a pimped version of the kiddie rides you see in shopping malls or outside supermarkets. The very first simulators, which were developed about a hundred years ago, were naturally quite simple affairs; today, however, they're true marvels of engineering, and can be used to super-authentically recreate real flight scenarios. Each type of plane has its own simulator. If, when flying for a commercial airline, you switch to a model you've never flown before, you first need to undergo a "type rating," which is kind of like a mini training course (flying might be freeing, but we're tied up in a lot of official jargon, too). There's a theory component, and then the practical component in the simulator, and only once you have the relevant type rating are you authorized to fly that particular aircraft type.

On this occasion, however, our simulator flight was not part of a type rating; it was to complete our training. I was amazed at how realistic it felt to fly in the simulator. Having spent months flying in nothing more than the yogurt cup or other light aircraft, I found the cockpit of the A320 utterly mind-blowing. I wished I could have started working as a pilot right there and then.

A graduation dinner in October 2009 finally marked the end of our training, and we joined graduates from two other courses in collectively celebrating this. I don't think I was the only one to have mixed feelings. On the one hand, I was proud of what I had achieved. At just twenty-one, I was essentially cleared to embark on a career as a pilot. On the other hand, this was now the start of a phase of uncertainty for most of us: Before we could get going with our career, we had to write applications—and wait, and hope. Coupled with this was the fact that the last eighteen months had seen several friendships forged between course participants. What would happen to these now that we would no longer be seeing each other every day?

The dinner was capped off for me with an award I hadn't expected: I had topped the class in the written LBA exam—something I only found out that night. As a reward, my flying school invited me to sit in the cockpit of an Avro jet—a short-haul British Aerospace passenger jet—on a flight from Frankfurt to Zurich. It was my first time sitting—and then actually taking off—in the cockpit of a plane that size.

CHAPTER

MINIMUM FIVE YEARS' EXPERIENCE, NEW GRADUATES WELCOME: THE JOB SEARCH

As part of my training, I had flown 210 hours, and completed a tidy 258 landings. I was now eligible to work as a First Officer (FO) on a commercial airline. Those of us who had invested in private training, however, were now not only a good US$80,000 poorer, we were also at a disadvantage when it came to the job search, because the number of flying hours we had so far recorded would not be enough to land us a gig at most of the major airlines. They require a minimum number of flying hours that it is impossible to have achieved as a new graduate. It was often four times what I had in my flight log—some even demanded a minimum of 4,000 hours. This was a lot, even in intercontinental-flight terms. A few airlines, like Condor and Germanwings, in turn, actually preferred new graduates, because it enabled them to mold the newbies to their needs. But, of course, those jobs advertisements would have dozens of applicants responding to them. In any case, the labor market for pilots didn't look particularly good in late 2009.

So, I was well aware the job search could be a long and tedious affair. It would take luck and patience. But I hadn't expected it to take quite as long as it did. I applied to more than forty companies right across Europe. The companies that still asked for hardcopy applications received high-quality portfolios. For many others, however, I was not able to make my submission stand out, because all applicants had to fill out the same online masks. My frustration grew with every rejection, though I was at least able to earn a little money on the side as a model at Germany's first Hollister store. It was also a welcome distraction from my job-search frustrations. But I wanted to fly, not just do parade laps.

This period of waiting and doing nothing (well, not doing what I wanted to do) felt like an eternity. After several months, I decided action had to be taken, so I researched courses that fit my interests. I soon found something that appealed to me: the international Aviation System Engineering and Management course for commercial pilots. (In German, this had the abbreviation—yes, another one—of ILST; if our industry had to communicate without abbreviations and acronyms, we'd never make it into the air with all the long-winded jargon.) Although studying was not exactly high on my wish list, I applied for a place at Bremen University of Applied Sciences. This would enable me to further expand my theory knowledge.

I was, indeed, soon accepted, and was advised the starting date of the 2010 winter semester. It wasn't what I had been hoping for, but it was better than nothing. What really annoyed me, however, was that my license for multi-engine planes would expire in June if I didn't fly before then. To renew it, I would have to complete additional flying hours, and fork out the equivalent of yet another US$1,000. Going to college now meant definitely not flying again for the foreseeable future, and I was scared my pilot career plans would have to be shelved.

My father could tell I was frustrated and at a loss, and he eventually came up with the idea of accompanying me to the AERO aviation show in Friedrichshafen. AERO is the largest and most important trade fair of its kind in Europe, bringing airlines, aircraft manufacturers, and amateur pilots together all in one giant building. The idea was for me to take a look around and, in particular, get talking to the various companies' HR people. My father accompanied me, occasionally chiming in to say, as a means of promotional endorsement, that he had already done several charter flights with me as the pilot.

While this trick didn't end up working, his approach had generally been the right one. As in nearly all industries, using your connections never goes astray in aviation either, and I got chatting with a guy who ran a private jet company in Berlin.

I had already applied to it and been rejected, so I initially assumed there would be little point in talking to him. Nor was there any reason for me to be nervous—after all, it's not like they could reject me again. Safe in this knowledge, I felt pretty cool and calm about approaching him. The conversation was friendly and stimulating, and when he found out I had obtained my First Officer's license the previous fall, he encouraged me to send in my application. "I already did," I told him. "You guys unfortunately rejected me." That's not a problem, he quickly assured me; I should just reapply. He would then personally ensure I was invited to Berlin for an interview. My spirits soared! As soon as we got home, I prepared a second application to the company and sent it off.

I was absolutely stoked about this second chance. Private aviation was the exact industry I wanted to break into. (Or should I say, "land into"?) The alternative would be a job at a commercial airline. Sure, you generally flew larger planes at those companies, but I had gotten it in my head that I wanted to get a glimpse of the more glamorous worlds, and jet around the globe with the rich and famous. I could always switch to a commercial airliner at some point—I would have notched up all the necessary flying hours by then. But for now, this job would be perfect for me. More adventurous and unpredictable, I was sure, than a job as a commercial pilot flying German vacationers to Mallorca or the Canary Islands five times a week. So, if they were going to invite me to Berlin now, I was going to impress them. Of that, too, I was very sure.

It didn't take long to get a response: "... we regret to inform you ..." Rejected! I came crashing back to earth. (Oops! ... I did it again.) I was crushed and angry. Why had that guy gotten my hopes up, only to turn me down again? I knew our conversation hadn't been a job offer, but I could at least have been invited for an interview. What a deflating waste of time. If that had been his idea of humor then ... no comment.

My cell phone rang barely five minutes after the rejection email had come in. It was a lady from the Berlin flying company whose rejection letter was currently open on my screen. She was sorry; she had made a mistake. Her boss had told her he had already arranged for me to come to Berlin for an interview. So, I was to disregard the rejection, and excuse her for the oversight. Talk about a roller coaster of emotions—albeit ending on a positive note. I started rejoicing as soon as I hung up.

Ten tips for your application

At this point I'd like to offer a few tips about writing applications. Clearly, I wasn't very successful at the start, but after ten years in the industry, I now know what you need to bear in mind. Plus: I get to make another list!

1. If at all possible, find out who your contact person is at the company, then address this person by name—it sounds a lot better than the tedious "Dear Sir/Madam." The best way to find out the name of your contact person is to call up the company. You may even be able to speak to the relevant person directly beforehand. Even better. In your covering letter, you can then mention this by saying, "With reference to our telephone conversation on 12/24/2020..."

2. Do your qualifications fit the job description? If you're not sure what exactly the requirements for the job are, ask the company, making sure your questions are as specific as possible. This will show the company that you really have read the job advertisement carefully.

3. Hardcopy portfolios are eye-catching, but most HR departments now prefer paperless applications by email. If the job advertisement doesn't clarify whether applications need to be in hardcopy or digital form, ask.

4. When it comes to digital applications, the file format is hugely important. Every HR officer will facepalm if you send them five Word files in a zipped folder. PDF files are generally the standard these days for digital applications. Ideally, put your covering letter, resume, references, and other documents in a single PDF file, ordering them in the sequence you would use for a hardcopy portfolio. Make sure the file is an acceptable size. Under no circumstance should you send attachments larger than 10 MB. For hardcopy applications, it's worth investing in high-quality portfolios.

5. While no employer can technically reject your application for not having a photo (or for only having an unflattering Polaroid taken by your best friend at your last house party), it's still common practice to provide the potential employer with a picture of you. Invest in good photos taken by a legit photographer, showing you looking as friendly, open, and professional as possible.

6. Using Comic Sans as a font in applications is obviously a no-no. In general, your application should be laid out in a clear, uniform manner. While an application is not the right place to go fully artistic, a few subtle, creative elements will help you stand out from the crowd. Use the company's color scheme in your letterhead, for example, or work the company's motto into your text.

7. The HR person doesn't want to know everything about your life history. The highlights of your last pub crawl have no place in your covering letter, which needs to be concise and precise, but still informative. Using as few sentences as possible, tell them why it's worth inviting you to an interview. Also make sure your spelling and grammar are 100 percent correct. Ask someone to proofread it all before you send it off.

8. If possible, list a few "hard facts" on a cover sheet, which will also feature your photo. These should be about five, max seven, points highlighting your strengths, which may help you stand out from the other candidates. It will allow the HR department to see, at a glance, what sets you apart. Use succinct dot points (bullets, not numbers) here rather than full sentences.

9. If you don't receive a response to your application, you can follow up by telephone after a little while. Timing is key here. If you call too early, it looks like you're hassling them, but it also looks weird to only follow up six months later. In my view, you're within your rights to pick up the phone after seven to ten working days and politely ask if your application has been received.

10. As mentioned above, my first application-submitting marathon was pretty frustrating. Don't let rejections discourage you, and, above all, be patient. Sometimes the road to your dream job can take a little longer than you think.

Wheels up for a new life

Following a successful interview in Berlin, and then also going through an in-person screening process to prove I could handle the aircraft types used, I received the long-awaited letter of acceptance. If I wanted, I could be part of their team. I now had to decide: studies or job? In the end, there wasn't much to think over. I had already decided against studying right from the outset by doing my pilot training. The letter of acceptance from Bremen that I had up my sleeve was my Plan B. But I had now finally found a way of achieving Plan A. I stepped up to the plate and opted for the job. This meant I now had to get the type rating needed to fly the Citation XLS. The training was held in London. The fun only lasted two weeks, but cost a handsome US$22,000, half of which I had to pay myself. Fortunately, the other half was covered by my local employment agency.

The first time I saw the plane, however, I must admit I was a little surprised. I had imagined it to be considerably bigger. If you think of private jets, you're more likely to think of luxurious cabins, with a king-size bed on the left, a Jacuzzi on the right, and an Italian fine-dining restaurant at the back—okay, maybe I'm exaggerating now. But the Citation XLS was definitely more XS than XL. The interior design was pretty special though: six pale leather seats—thickly padded and super-comfy—plus wood paneling and glinting gold trimmings made for a sophisticated vibe. In addition to the six passenger seats, there was another two-seater at the front, side-on to the cockpit, providing room for a stewardess to sit. At the back was a toilet cubicle—and, directly opposite, another small emergency seat that customers would no doubt have baulked at having to use. The cockpit, meanwhile, was surprisingly cramped. I had always imagined walking into the cockpit with my chic pilot's case—but there was absolutely no room for the thing. Most of the space was taken up with countless folders full of flight maps. (These days, they're all saved digitally on a tablet—hooray for technical advancements!) If the pilot and copilot squished together on the seat, there may perhaps have been enough room for a water bottle and banana as an emergency ration, though the Citation XLS had a large cargo hold for food and refreshments anyway.

Ultimately, I didn't care how big the plane was. I was just dying to finally get going. Having waited three quarters of a year, a completely new stage of life was now about to begin for me. I had been given clearance for takeoff into adulthood—now all I had to do was get the plane airborne. The Berlin-based job naturally also meant I had to move cities, and I was fortunately able to rent a small apartment from one of my godmother's friends in the Schöneberg district. So, using my connections got me a good start on the housing market too. I additionally had to wait for the license I had obtained as part of the type rating in London to be issued. The office in charge, which had also conducted the examinations in Zadar, was located in the city of Braunschweig (a.k.a. Brunswick). Licenses normally took about a week to issue, so when I had still received nothing after three weeks, I followed up. The licenses were issued by different people based on the licensee's last name, and it turned out the person responsible for the Bs was on vacation. The lady on the telephone was very helpful, delving deep into the mountains of folders that had apparently piled up on her coworker's desk. "I found you right at the bottom," she finally said. "You could have ended up waiting another four weeks. But I can sort it for you now." Yes, please! Absolutely. I decided to get in my car and drive straight to Braunschweig. Not even two hours later, I had the license in my hot little hands at last. I took a box of chocolates with me for the lady who had been so nice and helpful.

My first duty—with the tottering Shakira, the meatballs, and the client who appeared a day late—ended up being pretty weird. But I still felt like a pig in clover in my new life as a pilot, and I soon also made friends with my coworkers. I have always been a cheerful person, and fit in well in the team. Years later, a coworker recalled how I became "everybody's darling" in no time. Well, at least I made the effort to give a good account of myself. I was quick to help out wherever I could, and the female cabin crew in particular appreciated this when I took charge of loading and unloading heavy luggage for them.

The no-hassle package:
Let us take care of it

As our crew were "just" staff, we didn't usually get to see a lot of the glamour. But in my years as a private pilot, I did still get to experience a new world. The world of the jet-set crowd, which was as thrilling as it was absurd. When someone pays a few thousand euros for a ninety-minute flight, you know they're going to expect a certain level of service. But our clientele's idea of "normal" was often already pretty lofty even without the plane. Many took it completely for granted that they would be calling all the shots. The company went to great pains right from the outset to ensure no client was ever put out in any way—so the next one would be sure to be paying an equally large sum to fly with us. To make things even more difficult, our sales department tended to literally anticipate these clients' every wish and whim in order to secure a deal. A marriage proposal above the clouds? Not a problem with our no-hassle package—with champagne, of course. If they still want a stewardess to be there to open the champagne despite the rather intimate occasion, it's just a question of price. Rose petals scattered around the cabin? We can do that too!

These sorts of flight orders were usually forwarded to us with little or no comment. The sales department had done its job and was sitting pretty by then: The flight had been sold, and promises made to cater to every special request. The crew was left to take care of the rest. So, in addition to flying, we were also responsible for procuring and chilling the champagne and scattering the rose petals. Then comes the question of which flower petal merchant has enough rose petals in stock. Is selling rose petals even a thing? And if, on the day of the flight, fresh rose petals are delivered instead of the dried ones ordered, it still all seems very romantic at first glance. Things only get problematic when the bride-to-be starts tottering through the cabin in her stilettos, driving the petals into the carpet with such resolve that it simply has to be thrown out at the end.

Now, anyone who thinks this is just a matter of replacing a few square feet of carpet obviously isn't familiar with the special requirements of the aviation industry. This is not a problem that can be resolved by heading to your local discount furniture store. You need special products that have been tested and approved for the aviation industry. The materials used must particularly be flame-retardant and lightweight. The additional costs for this romantic gimmick alone ended up being around US$11,000—approximately five times my net monthly wage at the time. Yet most of our clients wouldn't bat an eye at an amount like that. (US$11,000 not enough for you? A stewardess once accidentally wrecked the microwave in the galley—that's the kitchen onboard a plane—by putting a metal spoon in it. The cost to replace the broken microwave? US$23,000.)

The flight I'm talking about here wasn't just memorable for the trampled rose petals. In addition to the captain and myself, our crew consisted of the aforementioned stewardess whose presence the client had expressly insisted on. (Airlines are not obliged to provide crew on small private flights, but more on that later.) Providing a stewardess is of course not the kind of special request that's difficult to fulfill. But as the client was going for a grand, romantic gesture, we began wondering how this stewardess would be able to provide the loved-up couple with top service AND the necessary privacy. Her seat was inside the cabin, and even if she stared at the side wall of the plane while sitting there, it would still have been impossible for her not to notice what the passengers were doing. Her only real task was to serve the champagne at the appropriate time. The client could naturally just as easily have procured this himself, but probably just wanted to prove to his beloved that, even in this respect, he had not stinted.

So, no problem; the stewardess opened the champagne. For the rest of the flight, however, the couple went to great—in some cases even drastic—lengths to convey that they didn't want to be disturbed, and this brought the stewardess to her knees in the truest sense of the word. As she was not able to sit in the crew seat—where would she have looked?—and there was no other separate staff area, she had to improvise. Which is why, at nearly 35,000 feet above ground, she knelt in a very uncomfortable position between me and the captain, being sure to keep her gaze duly fixed ahead of her at all times. Meanwhile, the newly engaged lass was endeavoring to thank her future husband for the wonderful surprise. She swiftly unlocked her hidden treasure and put it to good use at an altitude of over 36,000 feet—more or less hands-free. I'd have loved to tell them to "get a room!" because it was simply impossible to ignore what they were up to. But they probably figured a private plane is better than a hotel room when it's just a quickie. Or perhaps they were simply aiming to join the exclusive Mile High Club, whose single membership criterion—as everyone in the industry knows—is to have had sex in a plane.

As reckless as this behavior was, the mindset of many of our clients was indeed one of, "I've paid, so I can do whatever I like here." It occasionally made for a particularly exciting or unusual assignment, and the best-case scenario was that you would end up with a cool story you could later recount to your coworkers. (We were, of course, contractually obliged to keep these absurd tales among ourselves.) But you did sometimes have to wonder how people could act so brazenly.

Some of my coworkers once flew a DJ who openly smoked a joint onboard. He didn't pay the slightest mind to the fact that the smoke was wafting into the cockpit. It made the copilot sick, but the client obviously didn't stop to consider, even for a second, whether or not his behavior was appropriate, revealing an attitude that, in the worst-case scenario, could have put both him and the crew in real danger. This sort of thing really gets on my nerves. Next time, how about just doing a line of coke in the onboard toilet instead, mister. At least that doesn't impact everyone else.

I personally once had the pleasure of flying one of the best-known DJs in Germany, Paul Kalkbrenner, who gave me no cause for complaint. He was a nice guy who promptly invited our crew to his concert in Rome, which is where we were taking him. Not only did he get us backstage passes, he also invited me up on stage with him. There I was, standing in front of thousands of people in a giant arena, throwing huge plastic balls into the audience.

Europe's finest airports

So, there were constantly experiences that restored your faith in humanity when other clients and their crazy whims had given you reason to doubt it. In my first few months on the job, I was pretty sure I had hit the jackpot. I was traveling around the world. Before long, at just twenty-two years of age, I had been to more countries than my grandparents had in their entire lifetimes. It would often take me a minute or two to work out where I had just come from and where I was at any given time. Spain? France? Italy? Things can start to get confused when you're flying to each of these countries several times a week. Our most frequent destinations were jet-setter hubs like London, Paris, Zurich, Nice, Warsaw, and Berlin.

Nice is definitely one of the European airports I most love flying to. Not because the airport itself is particularly appealing or clean or otherwise well organized; it's unfortunately not. But the approach is spectacular. As a private-jet pilot, I often had the pleasure of landing there multiple times a week. Coming from the north, you first fly over high mountains, before descending toward the sea. In the best-case scenario, you fly over or even past Monaco, where, so as not to disturb the rich and famous in their luxury villas, a special approach has been devised, which involves flying primarily over the sea. For us, this meant initially approaching the runway at a 90-degree angle, before turning in and lining up for the final approach. This had to be done manually, using VFR and without autopilot. It was especially spectacular when you flew parallel to the beach and could see the swimmers down below.

Oslo soon became one of my favorites in terms of the airport—I mean the actual building—itself. The roof of the departure lounge is an elegant timber-and-glass structure that seems to float above you. Classic Scandinavian design; subtle yet extremely stylish. There are few other airports I can think of that are so well looked after. Everything is always sparkling there. The staff are extremely friendly, and the distances you have to walk are nice and short—another advantage when you're flying on a daily basis.

London Farnborough airport, which is only used for business aviation, is another pretty magnificent sight. The futuristic building was even used as a film set for the James Bond movie *Quantum of Solace*, showing off its impressive acting skills; it played the role of the fictitious Austrian airport Bregenz, and did so very convincingly.

But Austria didn't even have to pretend it had amazing airports, because Innsbruck was soon also added to my list of favorites. Admittedly, like Nice, it's more the approach that makes Innsbruck such a highlight for pilots. Taking off and landing there in clear weather provides a great view of Austria's mountains, though it is also very challenging.

The procedures are different, the mountains very close, and the runway not exactly the longest. Strong winds can cause turbulence, making things a little unpleasant for passengers. Another good thing about Innsbruck airport, however, is the fact that distances inside the terminal are short, both for crew and passengers. Within a few minutes of landing, you can be right outside the terminal building.

The Swiss airport of Samedan, near St. Moritz, also provides a magical backdrop for takeoffs and landings, with lush green meadows, dark forests, and a clear-blue river flanked by a mountain range. I often went there during my time as a private-jet pilot, flying celebs around during the winter. Samedan is also Europe's highest airport. It sits about 5,500 feet above sea level, with both sides of the high valley surrounded by mountains soaring to heights of more than 10,000 feet. This makes Samedan a challenge even for experienced pilots, and it can only be flown into in clear weather, because you need a minimum of visibility in order to take off or land there.

The second tragedy and the old chestnut of air safety

Samedan is sadly also the airport I associate with the second tragedy of my piloting career. It was where two of my coworkers suffered fatal crashes not long after I had met them. I had only been flying for the company for six months, and the crash in Zadar, in which a fellow trainee and an instructor had lost their lives, had barely happened two and a half years prior. Our company was to fly a client from Samedan to Rome a few days before Christmas. The flight was booked for the Monday morning, but my coworkers decided to fly to Samedan from Zagreb, Croatia, on the Sunday, a day earlier. It was an empty-leg flight, meaning no other passengers would be on board. In hindsight, you'd have to say that's what saved our company, which understandably came under great scrutiny from the aviation safety authority during investigations into the incident.

My coworkers were on approach into Samedan at around 3 p.m. Presumably due to the weather-induced poor visibility— it was snowing that day—, they had to abort their first attempt at landing, going around instead. They flew a loop and prepared for a second approach, during which the aircraft crashed and instantly burst into flames. The jet cut through three power lines, though it wasn't clear whether that happened during the crash, or actually caused the crash in the first place. The crash site lay on the outskirts of the village of Bever, just 55 yards from the train station, and right next to the heavily frequented platforms of the Rhaetian Railway and a substation. There was a housing estate 110 yards away. So, if things had been even slightly different, the accident could have resulted in a full-blown catastrophe.

Many companies at the time neglected to prepare their staff for the very specific challenges associated with taking off and landing at Samedan. The airport itself didn't offer adequate training either. Like every crash, this one, too, was very thoroughly investigated by the authorities, though my boss, as the employer, managed to be cleared of all responsibility. I fully understand why he so vehemently insisted that the company was not at fault. It must have been quite a balancing act for him: On the one hand, he had to cope with the death of two staff members. But if, on the other hand, the investigations had found him guilty in any way, this could very quickly have resulted in his entire business shutting down. Above all, it was probably the fact that no passengers were onboard why we ultimately bore no direct consequences.

I would soon discover, however, that there were definitely indirect consequences: At the best of times, European airports often cast a particularly critical eye over private aviation employees and aircraft during security checks—we have an abbreviation for these too: SACA or SAFA checks—and this seemed to be even more noticeable after the accident. I can't, and won't, complain when it comes to air safety, but all this naturally made our everyday work even more complicated than it already was.

In the wake of this crash, just as I had done after the one in Zadar, I tried to see it as a learning experience, rather than let it unsettle me. I had now experienced two tragedies in my immediate environment very early on in my career, and in comparatively quick succession. Among the questions I'm repeatedly asked, one of the more common ones, especially back then, is whether I worry about those sorts of tragedies. I don't want to go into too much detail here. On the one hand, because I want the tone of this book to essentially be a light one, and on the other, because people's fascination with plane crashes, as understandable as it may be, always harbors an element of voyeurism. There's an air of media-driven disaster tourism about it that I do not wish to engage with—while still fully understanding that some people are interested in these sorts of stories. Plane crashes and disasters really are very rare, relatively speaking. (For example, some of you will no doubt have heard that 2017 went down in history as the safest year in civil aviation. There was not a single passenger jet crash anywhere in the world that year—an achievement for which Donald Trump took credit, even though nobody apart from him knows how exactly he contributed toward it. People had stopped asking questions long before . . .)

Statistics on how safe flying is, comparatively speaking, are dredged up every time a passenger jet crashes somewhere. These statistics don't lie. Car drivers, bike riders, cruise passengers, and even pedestrians are more at risk than frequent flyers. There were 3,018 recorded civil aviation plane crashes between 1945 and 2015. As a comparison: 106 passenger liners suffered accidents on the world's seas and oceans in 2012; at that rate, there would be 7,420 accidents over the same 70-year period. In 2014, there were nearly 2.5 million car accidents in Germany alone, with more than 300,000 of these causing physical injury. Advocates of introducing speed limits on Germany's Autobahns are constantly cried down by the automotive industry and its supporters, who claim it's a constitutional right to tear up the road at 140 m.p.h. In aviation, meanwhile, every accident—justifiably!—results in discussions on whether existing safety mechanisms are adequate. These debates are necessary, and have helped our industry continuously improve its safety over the years.

Part of the reason plane crashes are covered in much greater detail by the media compared to car accidents is that they are more spectacular: There are more victims, the process is more dramatic, and, though flying itself has been one of humankind's age-old dreams, the fear of a potential crash triggers a primal fear of sorts in many people. While I myself have indeed experienced a few hairy situations, I always knew I still had control over them. As much as incidents like my coworkers' crash in Samedan rock you to your core, fear is not a good guide—particularly not for people who are responsible for the lives of many others. Of course, aviation accidents concern me, but I also take a professional stance here, and ask myself: What went wrong? What errors were made, and how can I avoid them?

CHAPTER

 4

WE DON'T EXPECT ANY TURBULENCE; PLEASE HOLD ON TO YOUR WALLETS

It is, of course, little surprise that, in an industry like private aviation, you come across clients with a long list of special requests—and we really did make every effort to duly fulfill these. Incidentally, it's not necessarily the stars and starlets who expect the world. For example, I once had the pleasure of flying Lady Gaga—but there are no juicy details to this story, because, on boarding the plane like the global star she was, she promptly slumped into her seat, pulled off her wig, and spent most of the flight sleeping. I figure people of that level often know exactly who they are, and don't need to continuously prove it to the rest of the world. In many cases, however, we didn't even know the names of our clients; they were high-ranking people from major companies, or those who had simply inherited their wealth. These were often the ones who would play to the gallery with preposterous special requests, and generally only bark orders at you. People who considered it superfluous to acknowledge others, not even with a "hello" or "goodbye."

Don't get me wrong: Our clients were paying the equivalent of several thousand dollars for a single flight, so their expectations were suitably high. I've never had a problem with doing my utmost to deliver top service. For most of our clients, however, chartering a private jet was more of an ancillary expense—like when we ordinary mortals splurge on a taxi instead of using means of public transportation. But when we do that, we're only buying the taxi ride—not the taxi driver as well.

Many of our clients' crazy whims were harmless and could easily be catered to. One gentleman, whom I always referred to as the "Vampire" would absolutely insist on all of the plane's windows being darkened before he entered the cabin. But that was his only request, so it was easy for us to satisfy it. He was actually one of the very few to give a tip. It was something I quickly had to learn in my job: Tips are anything but a given when you're flying the ultra-rich around the world. At the start, I was under the naïve impression that, if someone like me gave taxi drivers a few dollars as a tip, stars and CEOs with bulging bank accounts would almost certainly dig a little deeper to show their appreciation. Fifty euros (about US$56) per crew member seemed realistic to me. If you did thirty-odd flights a month . . . I calculated I would be able to afford a Porsche within six years—purely from money earned through tips. It wasn't to be. The Vampire was one of the notable exceptions, and the Porsche naturally never happened. (Not to worry: I now no longer have a car, and would invest the money elsewhere anyway.)

To be sure, the rich and the superrich haven't acquired their wealth by giving tips left, right, and center as they strut through life. Many of them have always been scrooges who shut their wallet as soon as the flight has been paid for. They probably figure, not wrongly, that there's no need for tips because, after all, the staff costs are included in the price. Yet a tip is also a token of appreciation, not a form of remuneration per se, and it's precisely those people who think the world revolves wholly and solely around them that are most stingy with showing any gratitude.

I incidentally later found out that some clients do indeed give tips—albeit at the time of booking the flight. The money is obviously just sitting in a company account somewhere, because we sure as heck never saw any of it. Another memorable flight was one that involved a passenger who had been stopped at border control because he was carrying more cash than allowed. The permitted amount was 10,000 euros per person, whereas this gentleman had a total of 11,000 euros on him. You couldn't count it like that, he explained to the security staff, because 1,000 euros were a tip for us. So, he was waved through, we flew him to his destination, and, when he disembarked, he said goodbye and disappeared without even mentioning the "promised" tip. "Hold on to your love," sang German rock band Ton Steine Scherben; for most of our clients, the love they held on to was simply their beloved money.

Someone who was somewhat more willing to open his wallet was a now deceased German entrepreneur we often flew around. We'll call him Mr. G. Having separated from his wife, who was nearly thirty years his junior, Mr. G. enjoyed using his wealth to go on little excursions with a varying array of lovers. I once flew him to the Oktoberfest in Munich. Onboard was a young woman, with whom he was obviously having an affair, and her mother, who herself was probably younger than Mr. G. We set off bright and early, at 7 a.m. As we wouldn't be returning until 8 p.m. that night, the crew needed somewhere to rest between flights. This is what is known as a "split duty," where the assignment can be officially split into two shifts. So, once landed, we headed to a hotel near the airport. We were young and full of energy, so I agreed to the flight attendant's suggestion of going to the Oktoberfest ourselves. We quickly freshened up at the hotel, changed our clothes, and took a taxi to the festival. We were on our first fairground ride when my work cell phone rang. I called back as soon as I was back on solid ground. "Where are you guys?" my OPS (Operations) coworker asked. I was a little puzzled as to where she expected us to be. Would we be told off because we hadn't stayed at the hotel like good employees? "We're at the Oktoberfest," I answered, truthfully. "Why?"

As it turned out, Mr. G. was already on his way to the airport, wanting to be immediately flown back to Berlin. The captain had stayed at the hotel, so he could at least go on ahead of us and prepare the plane for takeoff. We, meanwhile, had to first get back, change, and check out—eventually arriving at the airport long after Mr. G., who just couldn't understand why, having paid several thousand euros, he was the one who had had to wait over half an hour. What made it an even worse faux-pas was that the gentleman was a shareholder in our fleet. It was one of those moments where you want to tell the client loud and clear: "You've bought the flight, not the crew." We had even given him instructions and our contact details beforehand, telling him that if he wanted to leave earlier, that wouldn't be a problem; he just had to give us a little notice so we could get to the airport. Instead, he advised his change of plans to the sales department, which of course in turn didn't think to back us up by letting him know he would have to factor in at least a bit of waiting time for such short-notice requests.

I find the "I've got money; I can do what I want!" mentality commonly displayed by wealthy people unsavory. Mr. G. was a notoriously impatient client who loved flaunting his wealth and affairs with much younger women. So it was hardly a surprise when he once had the presumption to make a highly questionable offer to a Polish flight attendant: If she got herself pregnant with him and bore his child, he would pay her 2,000 euros (about US$2,200) per month to raise the child. He made her this offer while sitting next to his current partner at the time. Honestly! What kind of person thinks they can just spit out their scummy thoughts like that with no filter?

Zero percent pleasure in the Blow Up Hall

There was another wealthy Polish businesswoman whom we flew around regularly. She was often accompanied by her much younger lover, and tended to become quite melodramatic, prompting our company's management to urge us to treat her with kid gloves and offer her the absolutely best service. Among her many assets was a hotel (more on that in a minute) that also provided her catering when she once hired us to fly the short route from Poznan to Berlin. She was ravenous, she told us right from the start. There was no flight attendant on this particular flight, so I personally served her the food once we had reached the set cruising altitude. The meal consisted of a selection of some twenty delicacies, each in tiny plastic bowls. A colorful mix of amuse-bouches, if you will. She was bewildered and also somewhat annoyed. What had we been thinking? She'd said she was really, really hungry and needed to eat some proper food. I very amiably explained to her that her hotel was the one that had provided the catering, as agreed at the time of the flight booking. Well, she had no comeback then, did she. She ended up eating only two of the twenty canapés. But she's still alive, so she didn't starve to death.

Her hotel had almost legendary status among my coworkers. Many of them absolutely raved about it, while others positively loathed it. To me, the name alone sounded somewhat dubious: Blow Up Hall 5050. I should mention here that things can sometimes get pretty sexy in our industry, with pilots chasing after young stewardesses, and young stewardesses wanting to hook a pilot. So my thoughts immediately wandered in this direction, and I probably wouldn't have been surprised if this Blow Up Hall had simply ended up being a more sophisticated brothel. Then, one day, I had the opportunity to ask the owner herself what the name meant. The "5050," she explained, was to remind people that life is always about finding a balance. In this case: 50 percent pleasure, 50 percent business. Okay, perhaps not the most profound philosophical insight, but we can let that slide. Blow Up Hall 5050 was a design hotel, as I discovered when, after some two years, I was finally able to stay there myself. The interior was markedly dark, and there were no room keys or room numbers. Guests were instead given a phone to access their room, to which they were guided after check-in. While there weren't really many rooms, all the corridors looked the same, so it was a good idea to properly memorize where your room was. One of our captains had no interest in playing these little games; he always insisted on getting a key, and would then mark out his door with a Post-it note. I think this was partly also due to the fact that he liked to have a few beers outside in the evening, and knew it would be even more difficult to find the right room at the end of it all otherwise . . .

There's no denying the rooms were stylish. When I finally stayed there for the first time, I was given a large room, with full black-and-white décor and some really edgy design ideas. Functionality, on the other hand, had not been given much priority. Sometimes, when showering, the water ran straight over the bathroom floor and into the room, prompting us to build makeshift dams out of towels. In any case, my first night there was neither pleasure nor business, but rather one giant "blow up." We had dinner at a restaurant, where I ordered a beef roulade. The price included some very unpleasant food poisoning that saw me spend the whole night on the toilet, going for broke from both ends. A really awful experience that ended in me being taken to hospital the next morning and put on a drip.

Go right back, I forgot something

Many of our clients knew how to exploit the privileges of their wealth, and, boy, did my job soon teach me that affluence and laissez-faire don't necessarily go together! Precisely how several of them make sure the service they have purchased fully meets their expectations was made clear to me by two ladies, who expressly insisted on having Evian water onboard. Not a problem in itself. Except that I had to procure this water in a very specific form—in small bottles only sold in French stores. So the water was imported and provided as requested, and yet the pair pointedly scorned it. None of it was ever drunk. What they did do, however, was unscrew the tops of all the bottles, then screw them back on again, before finally returning the bottles to their holder. This was obviously their way of making sure the crew replaced the bottles after every flight, whether they had been drunk or not. Yes, ladies, we did replace the bottles, and your little snitching game was not lost on me. We incidentally had to tip the undrunk water out at the end.

Additional flights that had to be made when a client had left something behind at home were a special form of decadence. Two particularly crass experiences have stuck with me, and both involved Polish businessmen. The first, who was one of Poland's richest men, had hired our company to fly him, his wife, and their two daughters to their vacation destination. I wasn't the one hired, mind you, because I didn't have the type rating required to fly his private jet. He flew a silver Gulfstream G550, whose interior had been designed by Versace, and the famous head of Medusa synonymous with the Italian fashion label was emblazoned on every headrest of the ultra-comfy leather seats. I only ever had the pleasure of seeing inside the plane on one occasion—and it can rightfully be called the Rolls Royce of private jets. If you happen to come across US$57 million hidden away inside your sofa next time you clean your house, I would definitely recommend thinking about buying one. It's worth it.

The man also owned a helicopter, limousine, and luxury yacht. All these, just like the Gulfstream, had the same black-

and-white Versace interiors. That, ladies and gentlemen, is what you call decadence.

Upon arrival at their destination, however, he realized his precious daughters' bikes had been left at home in Poland. Obviously not wanting to have to deal with his princesses' disappointed faces, he quickly called our company and ordered an empty-leg flight to his hometown. So, we flew to Poland to collect the bikes, load them onto the plane, and send them off on their way to the vacation destination. I initially thought this was total madness. The client was paying a tidy US$23,000 extra for the whole exercise; he could have bought a whole fleet of kids' bikes at his destination for that price. Probably even with Versace-designed trimmings for a small surcharge. But a little googling and applying the rule of proportions soon helped me understand his thought processes: It was the equivalent of me spending about 50 cents. In other words, peanuts.

The other experience also came at the hands of a Polish businessman, whom we'll call Mr. L. He had hired us to fly him to Olbia, Italy. No sooner had we arrived than we were told that, instead of us having the night off as planned, another flight had been booked to Zurich, and then back to Olbia. The client was our dear Mr. L. We called to make sure there hadn't been some sort of misunderstanding; after all, we had only just flown him to Olbia. Well, it turned out he had left his cigars behind in Zurich. He seriously sent us back to fetch them. We boarded the plane, flew the ninety minutes to Zurich, and waited for someone to bring us the cigars, before flying another ninety minutes back to Olbia, where the precious cargo was handed over to Mr. L.'s chauffeur, who then delivered them to his client.

It was a mystery to me whether Olbia's fine array of premium tobacconists were too ho-hum for Mr. L.'s nuanced tastes, or whether it simply hadn't occurred to him to buy a replacement there. I later found out the cigar brand was one only sold in Milan, and it was obviously very important to him that his acquaintances saw him smoking this particular brand. He didn't seem to comprehend that the whole exercise was financially idiotic, not to mention had a devastating environmental impact. Imagine not hesitating to charter a private jet just because you've left your smokes behind; simply shrugging off five-figure costs because money plays no role (or should that be no Rolex?). In any case, that's exactly the type of people you'll find in Olbia.

Olbia's catering mafia

If you've never heard of Olbia, you're not alone. Before my first flight there, I had no idea the place existed. Yet the town, with a population of barely 65,000, ranks alongside London, Paris, Zurich, and Nice as a jet-set hotspot. The Italian municipality of Olbia is the fourth largest city in Sardinia, and is located on the island's picturesque north-eastern coast. Over time, the wealthy have turned it into an exclusive vacation destination by ensuring mere mortals simply cannot afford to stay there. One area of the airport is reserved for private jets. It is directly adjacent to the "normal" airport, which is not much more than a little taxiway and shabby terminal. Then suddenly, the vista opens out onto endless expanses, where private jets of all sizes sit alongside one another—from small planes like our Citation XLS to magnificent, palatial aircraft.

During high season, there will be around a hundred planes at Olbia airport. Of course, the rich and famous don't just have their own ramp area; they also have their own terminal, which, compared to the "normal" terminal, is a veritable haven of luxury. There's even a giant porch that private jets can easily park under to ensure their passengers are sheltered from the sun and rain when disembarking. Very rarely do you hear the words "airport terminal" and "grand" in the same sentence, but in this case it's true.

The rich-and-famous terminal doesn't trade on bargain prices for Absolut Vodka or Calvin Klein perfume. Patrons here prefer to shop for Chanel, Manolo Blahnik, or even Ferraris. If you want to treat yourself to a coffee and ice-cream after a session of duty-free shopping, be prepared to potentially be set back the equivalent of about US$170. For us, the bigger problem was the airport's "catering mafia": Food and drink couldn't be brought in from outside, but rather had to be purchased on site. They even charged more for dishwashing. It was highway robbery, and we dealt with it by improvising. We would smuggle a makeshift version of chilled sushi into the plane or stock up before flying to Olbia. We would occasionally sneak dirty crockery into the bathrooms so we could wash it in the basins there ourselves. While this was sometimes a little degrading, there was no other choice—unless you wanted to fork out US$1,700 on a simple lunch.

The airport staff—both the men and the women—were unbelievably attractive, but were neither competent nor friendly. The women tottered across the tarmac in skin-tight outfits and ridiculously high heels, barely able to keep their balance, leave alone help load and unload luggage with their long, painted nails. The majority would simply make a half-hearted apology for this in broken English.

Mr. L. often flew with us to Olbia. He took it for granted that we would wait for him. Everyone else had to fit in with his wishes and ideas, of course. He was there when he was there—and when he was there, everything had to happen instantly and seamlessly. We often waited hours for him, sweating buckets inside the plane as it got hotter and hotter—except for the captain, who was allowed to wait in the air-conditioned terminal. We had even bigger problems if we had to spend the night in Olbia. Mr. L. would step straight off the private jet and into his limousine, which drove him to his yacht, moored in the harbor alongside other luxury vessels. We, like all staff, had to stay in a pretty isolated, run-down hotel. I still remember my first time there. We arrived late evening, having put Mr. L. in his limousine and made the now overheated aircraft cabin sparkling clean. We were given a welcome cookie, but that was literally the only thing I was able to offer my grumbling empty stomach. There was no buffet, as the hotel restaurant had already shut. Room service prices were astronomical, and it would have been just as expensive for us to take a taxi back into the city to eat at a restaurant there. Meanwhile, Mr. L. was now probably lounging on his yacht's sundeck eating spoonfuls of caviar.

We were, of course, able to charge the hotel stays to the company, and we also received a daily food allowance of 40 euros (about US$45). That wouldn't have been enough for half an espresso at the airport, nor was it enough to buy anything else in Olbia. So I went to bed hungry that night, all the more excited about the breakfast buffet that was included in the room rate. Now Italians aren't exactly known for being big breakfast eaters; the classic Italian breakfast consists of coffee and a sweet pastry. But, the next morning, I stuffed my belly as full as I could without looking totally gross. I was generally getting used to behaving like my coworkers and making breakfast the most important meal of the day. The aim was to fill yourself as much as possible, because you never really knew when you would next be able to have a meal. This was particularly true in summer, when the number of last-minute assignments rose significantly. You may only have been rostered for a single flight in the morning, but four others might end up being booked throughout the day. It even got to the point where I would take filled rolls or bananas with me into the cockpit, which often prompted light-hearted teasing from my coworkers. But, hey, I was pretty much still growing.

We actually should have insisted on the company making sure we had an opportunity to eat and drink something. I mean, it was the rule. If nothing else to prevent dehydration and other physical limitations, employers need to ensure the crew is given the opportunity to have a meal and a drink during the Flight Duty Period (FDP). How exactly this is enforced is supposed to be detailed in the operations manual. You can say what you like on paper; the rules may have been laid out in the operations manual, but reality was very different. Here, too, it was all about cost-saving, meaning food wasn't usually ordered for us. Among the reasons given for this was the fact that flights were often booked last-minute, and that it was impossible to know beforehand whether we would be away, and for how long. My favorite reasoning was: "But you guys had an hour between flights. Why didn't you just grab something in the terminal?" Because, dear coworkers, an hour was barely enough time to clean the cabin, prepare for the next client, and refuel the plane.

Healing water and ALDI yoghurt

Let me just say a few more words about Mr. L., because he is definitely one of the more fascinating characters I experienced during my time as a private jet copilot. For example, he would have a whole series of special requests that had to be catered to whenever we flew him. This is why I sometimes also referred to him as "Mister Special" when talking about him to coworkers. One of his quirks was to insist on having a certain kind of healing water onboard. If we didn't have it in stock, I often had to do the rounds at various supermarkets before starting work until I found one that stocked it. He also needed to have his own thermos of hot and sour soup onboard. Also, of utmost importance was a specific variety of yogurt—and it really had to be this one particular brand. What kind of exquisite yogurt product must it be that a person of Mr. L.'s rank was requesting it? This was a man who knew all about the finer things in life. A man who would simply send a private jet from Olbia to Zurich because he had forgotten his cigars. When Mr. L. asked for yogurt, it absolutely had to be ALDI's home brand—because he had spent some time in Germany as a young student, and this yogurt obviously held a culinary and nostalgic significance for him. Even when we flew him from Olbia to Warsaw or Zurich, he had to have his beloved yogurt from ALDI Nord onboard, which wasn't always easy to arrange. But anyone who has his Gurkha cigars flown in is not going to hesitate to send a private jet for a few cups of ALDI-gurt either.

This sentimentality was seemingly at odds with dear Mr. L.'s appearance. The guy was nearly 6'5", with a frame to match; he had a boorish, angular face and a white-blonde crew cut. His manner was often very bossy and abrupt, which particularly intimidated one of our flight attendants who, like him, came from Poland. He was a billionaire there, but even if you converted his wealth from Złoty to US dollars, he was still worth a good 900 million. He was used to everyone literally being at his beck and call, especially said flight attendant. Though he had flown with her for several years, he never called her by her name; he simply gave a shrill whistle to indicate that her services were required. For him, respect was something he expected to be shown, but which he rarely showed others, particularly women. What was that thing that too much money is said to spoil again? Ah, that's right: character.

One of our flight attendants, Vivien, was tough enough to not put up with his cheek. With her direct, upfront manner and sharp Berliner tongue, she managed to politely but firmly put him in his place right from the start. His whistle resounded through the cabin, summoning Vivien to his seat. She came, looked at him in a benignly reproachful way, and said: "But Mr. L, there's no need to whistle. My name is Vivien, and you are welcome to use it when you want something." Mr. L. was both stunned and impressed, but respected her request; he never whistled for her again.

I had also been warned about him before I flew him for the first time. He was a very headstrong and particularly important client, I was told. I had started my job with a naïve optimism that led me to believe that every client was an important client—after all, they were all paying enormous sums for their flight. But Mr. L. was a regular client, so the company did everything it could to keep him happy. Heaven help us if the healing water, hot and sour soup, or ALDI yogurt wasn't provided! He would throw a fit at unforgivable mistakes like that. When he flew with employees, they were strictly prohibited from eating or drinking onboard. They would of course bow down to all his commands, yet when we flew these same employees without him, they would go hog-wild and order the crew around like no tomorrow. When the cat's away, the mice will play ...

The notoriously late Mr. L. eventually even managed to get us to keep to his own personal time zone. L-time was two hours plus, because he was always at least two hours late. Maybe his secretary didn't trust us either, which was why she always booked us two hours before the arranged time to ensure we were there when it was time to go. In any case, Mr. L. showed me very early on in my job what I could expect much of my work as a private-jet pilot to entail: waiting.

Empty tank, full client

This was also the secretary who had booked a flight for Mr. L. to Saratov, a city on the Volga, an approximately two-hour flight east of Moscow. At the best of times, flights into Russia's heartland were a new ball game. We flew into these airports quite regularly back then, and every time, we would find ourselves in a completely different world to the one we were used to. The elaborate procedures in place at European airports didn't apply here. Air traffic control didn't assign landing slots; instead, the golden rule was "whoever comes first, lands first." If several pilots were on approach simultaneously, you simply had to make sure you didn't get in anyone else's way. This sometimes meant having to fly around in circles waiting for a runway to become free—and it was the reason we only ever flew into those airports with tanks filled to the brim.

Arrival and departure checks, meanwhile, were significantly more rigorous in cities like Saratov. Every flight out of and within Russia had to be approved with a stamp and signature.

This was often a case of OTT bureaucratic nitpicking that could end up being a really long-drawn-out process. Coupled with this was the fact that you weren't even allowed to leave the plane without a visa, resulting in me (admittedly through my own scattiness) one time having to sit for five hours in a parked plane while waiting for a US$570 replacement for my day visa. On many occasions, our plane was searched from top to bottom immediately after landing to ensure we didn't have any illegal passengers onboard. Then, before departure, four or five guys with machine guns would sit in the cabin, monitoring everything until the very last minute to make sure we didn't smuggle anyone out of the country. As you can imagine, this was all pretty overwhelming and intimidating for a newly qualified pilot in his early twenties.

While the prices in these parts of Russia were perhaps not quite at Olbia levels, they were still exorbitant. The amounts they charged us to de-ice our small plane would have been enough to de-ice an entire Boeing 747 somewhere else. While money was a language people spoke fluently here, the airport staff's English skills were often nonexistent. It was not uncommon for us to communicate using Russian notes we had somehow managed to cobble together beforehand. My idea of cities like Saratov may have been shaped by clichés, but it was usually pretty close to the mark. The days were consistently drab; the weather was cold, gray, and unpleasant. You always felt a vague sense of being alone and isolated. The people didn't tend to be overly friendly, and would eye us up sullenly. The fact that the aviation industry's international practices and conventions didn't seem to figure here meant these flights posed a particular challenge for crew. As a pilot, it was a very useful learning curve, but I'm still pleased I no longer fly to this region.

In any case, that flight with Mr. L. I wanted to talk about was taking us to Saratov. Or should I say: The flight took us via Saratov. Mr. L.'s secretary had chartered a flight from Moscow to Saratov on Easter Sunday, which seemed strange to us from the outset. Given the vacation period, it would have been more obvious to fly to Gdansk. As it turned out, the secretary had indeed made a mistake. Suddenly, the announcement came that Mr. L. wanted to be flown straight to Poland—and, as usual, objecting was not an option. Within Europe, there wouldn't have been any problem logging a new flight route and catering to his request. But in Russia, we had no other choice; we had to fly the registered route. This meant first jetting two hours in the wrong direction to Saratov before being able to take the new route from Saratov to Poland. And as if all this wasn't already annoying enough, we had to disembark in Saratov, drive to the terminal, and present our ID in order to be granted permission to leave again.

I myself was allowed to stay onboard because I had to take care of refueling the plane. So, I just gave Vivien my passport, and therefore didn't personally experience the bus ride to the terminal and back. But Vivien's tales were epic enough: The floor of the bus, she said, was so thoroughly rusted that you could sometimes see the asphalt of the road pass by beneath you. There were no longer any doors. Mr. L., who had spent the whole flight over ranting and raving so much that Vivien had had to keep appeasing him with new rations of vodka, was now drunk out of his mind, and nearly toppled out of the beat-up bus on several occasions. Vivien, who herself could hardly believe she survived the ride, had her hands full trying to yank this colossus of a man back into his seat.

The stop in Saratov saw Mr. L. lose a good six hours and a whole bunch of money, and his mood was suitably foul. We could hear him constantly cursing and swearing. "Kurwa!" he kept shouting—a word that has various meanings in Polish, none of which are particularly complimentary. We'll assume he was using it in the sense of "f***ing hell," because that would be the most benign translation in this context. In any case, his violent rage left us fearing that his secretary would rather pack it all in than have to face him again.

Please, wait!

That she wasn't the only secretary to make a blunder of this scale would be proven on another occasion by our sales team. To ensure international communications are consistent, not only has the aviation industry established English as its official language of operation, but it also works on Coordinated Universal Time (UTC). (That's Central European Time, which is used in countries like Germany, minus one hour. During Summer Time it's minus two.) Our office would, of course, send bookings through to us in UTC, so we were somewhat surprised when Mr. L. ordered a flight to Warsaw with a departure time of 8 a.m. He really wasn't a morning person, and for us, it meant having to get up by no later than 5 a.m. So, we spent the night at an airport hotel, which is something we otherwise try to avoid. The only advantage of airport hotels is their fast access to the airport. Apart from that, they're honestly not ideal, because they're cut off from urban infrastructure, and have the added nuisance of aircraft noise.

While we knew full well Mr. L. would arrive at least two hours late, we naturally couldn't bank on it. So, we went through the torture of getting out of bed at 5 a.m. and making our way to the airport to prepare the plane and wait for our client. As expected, he didn't show up at 8 a.m. Nor had he appeared by 9 a.m.—also not much of a surprise, but one can always hope. When there was still no sign of him at 10, then 10:30, however, it started to get annoying. Somewhat exasperated, we called the office just before 11 a.m. to find out if they had heard anything. Our colleague from the sales team asked us to be patient. I mean, sure; what was another twenty-odd minutes after four hours of waiting. He then called back and explained that we had been called for an 8 a.m. start in error; it should have been 8 p.m. This was a totally inexcusable mistake, because UTC works on a 24-hour clock, unlike the twelve-hour clock used in standard written language in countries like the United States. Providing clear time information was part of our sales team's daily job. This sort of a mix-up was like me mistaking the galley for the cockpit.

But it's not as if moaning was going to help us either, so we went back to the hotel, where we booked a day room so as not to have to spend the next eight hours in the plane. The breakfast we had provided as catering for Mr. L. naturally had to be replaced with dinner, so we started preparing the plane again from 7 p.m. UTC. Then we had to wait, because of course we had to add the extra L-time onto the UTC. We waited until 9 p.m., then 10 p.m.—still no sign of Mr. L. Finally, despite the late hour, we managed to get more info from the office. Mr. L., we were told, had totally canceled the flight a few hours prior; they had forgotten to let us know. So, for the second time, we had come to the airport for no reason, and, again for the second time, had had to wait over two hours for nothing. Two faux-pas in a row, which meant we had been on call from 5 a.m. to 10.30 p.m., with absolutely nothing happening. Instead of an honest apology, we were then met with complaints about the fact that we had booked ourselves a hotel room again—because those were costs the company would like to have saved on.

Shady characters

Mr. L. lived in Gdansk and worked in Warsaw, and that route, in both directions, was consequently the one we flew most frequently with him. His business dealings were questionable to say the least, prompting the occasional investigation by Interpol. But this hardly limited his lavish travel regime. For one, he had multiple passports, meaning he could choose the identity he wanted to use when entering a country. He also often chartered multiple planes at the same time to cover his tracks. He always traveled with a black leather Louis Vuitton bag I had been eyeing enviously since the very first time I saw it. It was a real gem worth more than US$3,500. Whenever Mr. L. got out of the plane, the bag would be left onboard, which made me suspect it contained something he didn't want the border-control officers to see. If I had known what was in it, I would have volunteered to take the thing off his hands. I would never have dared ask him myself, but Vivien, who now had a good rapport with him, went about it with her usual assertiveness: "What's in that fancy bag you always carry with you, Mr. L.? It's so heavy." The answer: "100,000 euros." The equivalent of about US$115,000. It was his emergency reserve, so to speak, because you never knew when you would suddenly need a little cash.

In Poland, he seemed to be able to do as he pleased—he was considered a prominent businessman there. He also had excellent contacts within the Polish government, which had a financial and political interest in ensuring the justice system didn't call him to account for his shady financial activities. But he did have to be careful when traveling internationally. While it was certainly exciting to work for him, I could also have done without it. We were advised to turn a blind eye to Mr. L. and his wheeling and dealing, but I sometimes imagined what would happen if there were a dramatic shootout on the tarmac at some international airport—and me getting caught up among it. Fortunately, that never happened.

A flight with another dubious person could also have taken an interesting turn, but thankfully never did. We were going to Schönefeld airport to wait for our client and her four companions, whose names we didn't yet know. But as we arrived at the airport, the client was already waiting for us. "Your client is already here for the flight to Warsaw," said a terminal staff member, pointing to a smartly dressed, middle-aged lady. She was there far too early, but by now there was little that surprised us. The captain went over to her and introduced himself, and they chatted briefly, before the lady got down to business. She would head over to the plane in a minute, she said,but we had her permission to get going. We politely explainedto her that the departure wasn't booked for another hour; we still had to prepare the plane, and she was welcome to sit in the terminal lounge until then. But she didn't let this bother her. "Okay, be quick; I'll still come with you and wait in the plane."

Now, in a cabin as small as that one, you really don't want someone watching over you as you prepare things, so we once again very politely referred her to the lounge. But this made her all the more determined on coming with us. She was interested in aviation anyway, she told us, and would love to have a look at everything. We had no choice but to take her with us—the company didn't like it if we didn't cater to our clients' every wish. She actually turned out to be very friendly, even flirting a little with the captain, though he was nowhere near as well groomed as her. We worked as quickly as we could, but were hindered by the fact that she was already starting to order food and drinks. At one point, the captain asked when her companions were coming. "Nobody else is coming; I'm flying on my own," she told us. We wanted to make sure she hadn't made a mistake, because she had definitely booked for five people. "No, that's correct; I'm flying on my own." The captain found the whole thing kind of weird, and decided to call the office again. They promised to check it out, and called back soon after, advising that something wasn't right with the name, and asking us if they could speak to the client herself briefly. We passed the phone to her, and she had a quick chat with the sales team. She then handed the phone back to us and said, "All good; I've cleared it up. We can get going." She seemed in a little too much of a hurry, even though we weren't due to leave for another half an hour. The captain hadn't understood what the problem had been with the name either, so he called the office again: "So we can get going as soon as possible, yes? The client has said everything's in order." Panic at the other end of the line: "What? No! Definitely not! We told her she needs to leave the plane; she's not the client."

Even though it had now become clear there was some foul play going on, we kept things very friendly and tried to convince the lady she was in the wrong plane. In the meantime, the sales team had informed the police, who arrived at the plane soon after. The actual client and her four companions eventually also appeared. It was quite an absurd situation. Finally, the police escorted the wrong client from the airport grounds, and we were able to set off on our flight to Warsaw, which she had unsuccessfully attempted to trick her way into.

A week later, she tried the whole charade again with a different crew. A quick bit of googling revealed an even weirder side to the story. The lady was a former German Olympic champion, who I suspect must have been a bit screwy in the head. On her second attempt, she was temporarily taken into police custody. To this day, I sometimes wonder what would have happened on that flight if we had believed her ...

Shadiness is only one step away from darkness, and things get pretty dark when I now try to google another client we regularly used to fly back then. It's simply impossible to find any information on him anywhere on the Internet. It's as if he's erased all traces of his existence. The man was a simple farmer from Turkey, who had bought land in Azerbaijan for a good price. But, for reasons unknown to me, the government took these estates off him, instead promising him different land to compensate for the expropriation. As luck would have it, he unexpectedly struck oil on this land, and became filthy rich overnight. Perhaps it's better Google can't help me refresh my memory of him, because whatever I can remember is highly unpleasant. For example, he would force the stewardesses to crawl around the cabin on all fours. Arias by Luciano Pavarotti had to be played as onboard music. We could live with that, but he had an epically violent temper. If something wasn't right, he would shout in barely comprehensible English, demanding for it to be fixed. Or he would take quick action himself. One time, he didn't like the cushions that were lying around in the cabin. We had already started taxiing along the runway, when he ripped the door open in rage and threw the cushions onto the tarmac. For air-safety reasons, if nothing else, this was absolutely insane behavior that caused considerable problems for our crew. But, as I later found out, he had a much, much more sinister side. He eventually went to court for child abuse, and disappeared behind bars for a while.

Stewardesses and mistresses

A former female colleague of mine similarly went into "hiding," if you like. Obviously in nowhere near as grim a way as the crazy oil millionaire. (But you've got to segue to the next story somehow, right?) Like many other stewardesses, she had primarily gotten into private aviation with the hope that, while flying above the clouds, she would meet a man with a big bank balance, whom she could then marry. And what better place to look for a wealthy Prince Charming than in a private jet, so close to (seventh) heaven, at thirty-six thousand feet above ground? This wasn't a totally stupid idea, and it sometimes even bore fruit. This certainly was the case for her. She ended up meeting a German businessman who asked her to marry him. He gallantly led her out of her stewardess' job and into her supposed calling of being a wife. Nobody knows whose classist snobbery was responsible for her then abandoning her old name. But not only did she take his family name; she also changed her first name so that nobody could trace her progression from lowly flight attendant to well-heeled wife.

As I said, she was far from the only one to set out with the intention of using her stewardess job as a springboard. "Steward(ess)" is not a legally defined professional title, and while cabin crew working for commercial airlines undergo extensive training to guarantee a certain standard in both safety and service, the stewardesses of private airlines often have no training that would necessarily qualify them for the job. Spend two or three years serving champagne and canapés above the clouds until Mr. Right one day plops himself down on the pale leather seat—that was the rough plan for many young women I have flown with over the years. These women's main qualification was being exceptionally attractive. The small cabin, coupled with the fact that our guests were cut off from the rest of the world for an hour or two (there was no Internet onboard back then), helped a lot, because this often quickly created an intimate atmosphere between stewardess and passenger, if that is what both parties wanted.

Flights with these types of coworkers always meant a bunch of extra work for me. Many clients, on the other hand, placed no emphasis on the stewardesses' professional qualifications. One of our regular clients chose his flight crew wholly and solely based on visual appearance. Over the years, our company had been able to get a really good idea of his taste in women, and frequently provided him with a little catalog containing a selection of suitable candidates. I found it pretty wrong that we had to endorse his sexist behavior, but many of the young women who found work with us this way didn't seem to mind in the slightest. Their attractiveness was their trump card, and they played it whenever needed. I personally think people end up selling themselves short with this sort of approach. "Marrying into money" shouldn't be anyone's top aim in life. For women in particular, it's almost like reviving the spirit of the 1950s and '60s, when businessmen with sizeable wealth (and girth) would marry their secretaries, one after another. Clearly none of my business, nor did I expect anyone to ask me for life advice; all I wanted was for the flight attendants to do their job properly.

In the case of another coworker, however, I could understand where she was coming from. She was a musician, and, when flying for us as a stewardess, would rarely be without her ukulele. After all, you never knew who was going to be onboard, and what opportunities there would be for her to advance her career. This was how she once met Sting. I don't remember where we were flying from or where we were taking him, but this coworker made the most of the relatively short flight time to play something for the global star and ex-singer from The Police. I always really liked her music, and she has now become such a successful musician that she has so far released four albums and had several million plays on Spotify. (I tried contacting her through various channels to ask if it was okay to mention her by name here, but unfortunately did not receive a response, so I can't promote her here. Much like the other coworker who changed her name, it seems this one, too, simply no longer wants to be associated with her past life as a stewardess.). Sting, for his part, was not overly taken with the effectively unsolicited performance—presumably less because he didn't like the quality, and more because he found her brazen move pretty inappropriate. As far as I know, he never flew with us again.

Rio. A fierce headwind. Hair sitting perfectly. And, of course, this selfie is 100 percent authentic . . . right? In any case, it reached more than 2 million. I like that.

@pilotpatrick

Right from a young age, I loved any form of transport. *Left:* on Grandpa Walter's motorbike (1989). *Below:* my first flight, from Frankfurt to Mallorca.

MALLORCA 90

Young Patrick once again enjoying an air show near Frankfurt. I must have been about four years old.

I was, of course, allowed to have the window seat: flying to Spain with my parents, 1991. Only three years old, but not at all scared.

Below: with Mom, Grandma, and Aunt Ju in the background. *Right:* me (10) with my brother and cousin at Frankfurt airport.

2008 was the year I began my pilot's training. Here I am sitting in the cockpit of an A340 during a hangar tour at Frankfurt airport.

From top to bottom: in the cockpit of a Boeing 747 with my brother Pascal; my fellow trainee Fabian and I during an emergency training course in 2008; in the cockpit of the "yogurt cup." *Above:* first solo flight in Zadar, 2008.

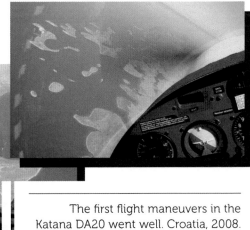

The first flight maneuvers in the Katana DA20 went well. Croatia, 2008.

The view was so cool, even my flying instructor was thrilled: second practical phase, flight over Miami Beach, 2009. Shortly after our "spy mission."

Vero Beach IFR training 2009 in the pilots' paradise of Florida.
Left: in front of the Piper Arrow. *Right:* flying with vision-inhibiting goggles and instructor Scott.

From top to bottom: excursion to the Kennedy Space Center; final practical phase in Zadar; 21st birthday in Palm Beach (all in 2009).

King of the air
and the waves:
jumping into
the blue Adriatic
Sea after passing
my final test.

Observer flight with Swiss as a
reward for outstanding performance.

Still no job, but already posing like a pro: during the application phase in 2010, in front of and inside a Falcon 2000 business jet.

Even simulated emergencies can get you sweating: type rating in Farnborough, UK (2010).

Below: first tentative attempts as a selfie artist. *Right:* first flight to Nice (hair looking good, pants less so).

First run in the Citation XLS . . . and a bunch of meatballs from catering for my first "real" flight.

Family onboard: I was finally able to take my loved ones on a flight to Innsbruck in 2015.

Above: Samedan airport. Stunning, but also a challenge for pilots.
Left: flashier than it looks— the terminal in Olbia.

That's not a yeti behind me; it's just the seat cover. Selfie time in the cockpit. Unfortunately not in shot: Venice.

Malta, 2015, out and about with my first action camera. Taking my first steps toward an Instagram career.

More fun as a trio: crew selfie with stewardess Dimi and captain Florian. Vibe and flight: both great!

"Ladies and gentlemen, this is your captain escaping."
A passionate aviation poser, in Cannes, France, 2016.

Left: in front of the Citation XLS.
Right: the cabin of the Embraer Legacy. It's nicer in the cockpit.

Refitted Boeing 747: a night in the STF Jumbo Stay is a unique Stockholm experience.

2019: my first duty as captain was preceded by simulator training.

Strong and colorful together: More diversity in the industry will drive aviation up again. Guaranteed.

We don't need a cleaner;
we've got a pilot

I myself have always been someone who values good service, whether as a customer or as a service provider. (Coupled with the fact that I was still a newbie to professional life and wanted to prove myself.) Our clients were shelling out several thousand euros at a time because they wanted to be comfortable and have maximum privacy when flying. While this may seem decadent or wasteful, it was important for me to give these people the best possible flight experience. It started with placing great emphasis on having a neat, well-groomed appearance and an unfailingly polite, customer-oriented manner. I would prepare the flights meticulously, position the client's requested extra cushions and snacks, and would often be the one buying the champagne or the drinks on my way to work. I would darken all the windows for the Vampire, and provide untouched Evian bottles for our bottle testers. I did an extra run to the nearest ALDI for Mr. L. on more than one occasion. Once the flight was over, I would ensure the plane was spick-and-span so that the crew taking over from us had no extra work to do.

I soon earned a reputation at my company. It was quite a good one, especially among the stewardesses—even if I do say so myself. They saw me as reliable, helpful, and a stickler for detail; after all, often enough, I did a lot of their work for them. But, as I gradually discovered, some of the pilots obviously found me too ambitious. My love of details was sometimes deemed too sissyish and effeminate. To this day,

I can't understand what's so womanly or, for that matter, manly about making an effort to do your job particularly well. For me, it was simple: We were servicing a luxury clientele—if you were only interested in offering service by the book and nothing more, you were in the wrong job.

It was stressful enough that the company was trying to save wherever it could. This sometimes became embarrassing, such as the time we flew one of the richest women in Germany—a client very heavily involved in social matters. The company had provided a selection of snacks like Hanuta hazelnut wafers and Milky Ways. Openly irritated, the lady asked me if she had mistakenly come to a child's birthday party. You couldn't really blame her, given her status. We could at least have thrown in a few Merci chocolate bars.

Alternatively, a bottle of red wine—any select drop—would of course have been nice. It reminds me of two businessmen who flew with us to Ukraine for the final of the Euro 2012 football championship. As they hadn't booked a stewardess, it was my responsibility to top up the drinks supply. We had water, soft drinks, tomato juice, and white wine, but were missing red wine. As luck would have it, I found a bottle in the store room—on the shelf used for expired food. (When I write it like that, it seems weird to me too. No idea why we had a shelf for expired food instead of simply disposing of it.) I had no clue how the bottle had gotten there, but I couldn't see an expiration date on the label, so I took it onboard. Just as well; because red wine was precisely what the businessmen ordered. Playing my steward's role, I enthusiastically read out to the gentlemen what was on the label: "Château Latour," I announced, my suggestive tone making it sound like a question. But I was met with a disinterested "yeah, yeah, that's fine." So I poured two small glasses—not too full—, left the rest in the bottle, and took my leave back to the cockpit. But, as was so often the case, only the two glasses were drunk; the rest of the bottle was left onboard when the men disembarked. As I have already mentioned, I do have a problem with food wastage, and there was also nothing to say we would be given anything to drink at the hotel later that evening, so I filled a small water bottle with wine to take with me. I tipped the rest of the wine out—there was still a good glassful left. Before disposing of the empty wine bottle, I took a photo of the stylish label. Who knows; perhaps I had discovered a decent new house wine.

That night in my hotel room, I was watching the football final when I remembered the wine. Curious, I drank out of the plastic bottle, but it honestly wasn't a case of love at first gulp. It's not that I knew much about wine, but it tasted to me like something you would disparagingly refer to as "cheap" wine. I didn't even finish it, preferring to just tip it out. Flicking through my cell phone photos once back home in Berlin, however, I stumbled across the label again, and did a quick Google search of what I had actually drunk. I nearly fell off my chair when I saw that this Château Latour, 2005 vintage, was selling for 1,500 euros (about US$1,700) a bottle. To this day, I have no idea how such a fine, expensive wine had ended up on our company's "leftovers" shelf, given the company's track record of cutting corners.

The company also saved money by not hiring cleaners before and after flights to spruce up the plane. That was left to the crew. Depending on which captain was on shift, it could also mean that the copilot was made the one responsible for cleaning. Nor was it beneath me to clean the toilet cubicles when this was necessary; it was definitely an aspect that hadn't been focused on enough in my training.

At the beginning, I was actually proud of the way I didn't hesitate to pitch in whenever a helping hand was needed. So, I would do the cleaning and shopping, and even serve food and drink if no flight attendant was on the flight. But I gradually came to the sobering realization that the company didn't give any brownie points for this extra work; it just expected us to take care of it. If I had been one to go by the book, I could have insisted on having the fifteen minutes of rest time after each landing that was stipulated for us pilots. Instead, almost every flight involved a good ninety minutes of clean-up time. Since I was "just" the copilot, I was often assigned the particularly unpleasant tasks. The captain, for example, would refuel the tank while I scrubbed the toilet bowl. It was in those moments that I realized how little we got to share in our guests' glamour. Not that our rich female client would have given it a second thought, but I'm pretty sure she would never have guessed that, after the flight, the young pilot in the smart uniform would swap his cockpit controls for toilet-cleaning rags.

It sometimes felt like I was doing two or three jobs at once. Flying made up maybe a fifth of my working hours. The rest of the time, I was a cleaner and flight attendant, delivery service, decorator, and solo entertainer. I also spent entire weekends updating approach charts. Every airport has these, and if you think of roughly how many airports there are in Europe, you can imagine how long it took to update a folder containing every European approach chart. (There are nearly 350 just for regular commercial airports; Germany has the third highest number, with twenty-eight, trumped only by Italy, with thirty, and Great Britain, with thirty-four.) So, I would toil away through seven bulging ring binders, laboriously folding the thin chart paper the correct way, and replacing the old charts with the new. It was awful! One time, I had just updated the folders in detail when they fell out of their holder and burst open during a takeoff, scattering hundreds of pages across the entire cabin. It took hours to put them all back into order, and, annoyingly, I only had myself to blame.

The takeoff had been part of an empty-leg flight, and when no clients were onboard, we often used the chance to get more out of the jet than would otherwise be possible. With the fuel tank half full, no luggage, and no passengers, our little Citation XLS actually had pretty impressive power. At takeoff alone, it could go from 0 to 125 m.p.h. in under fifteen seconds. We would then ascend more steeply than usual and reach an altitude of nearly 10,000 feet in just three minutes—meaning an average ascent of more than fifty-four feet per second. Once we had reached our cruising altitude, we would manually push the yoke forward to accelerate, the negative G-forces lifting us out of our seats. Top Gun, baby.

Or, as I would say these days: #aviationporn. Such were some of the particular pleasures we private jet pilots were able to enjoy. This sort of behavior would be unthinkable in a major airliner cockpit, if nothing else, because flight data is sent to the company in real time. The Flight Data Monitoring people would be onto you straight away. Safety first, baby. Or even: #aviationnorm.

No dessert for me, thanks

Whether they were good at their job or not, there was one advantage to flying with stewardesses. When staying over-night in foreign cities, it meant we would be a nice little trio, which usually made the evenings more entertaining than when it was just me and the captain. To outsiders, we must have looked quite strange, particularly as I was still new to the job. I was just twenty-two, the stewardess would be another two years younger, and our captain would barely be thirty. We weren't necessarily a combo you'd entrust a 15-million-dollar plane to. While we wore the uniforms, we were actually too young for people to buy the fact that we held the positions these uniforms represented. Some people probably thought we would be better suited to a carnival for kids. (And, if it was a good trip, we would end up enjoying ourselves as if we were indeed at a carnival for kids.)

But older coworkers sometimes had their own ideas of what constituted good use of free time. This became apparent whenever one of the captains commented that I hadn't yet been introduced to the true pleasures of aviation. It was a while before I found out what he meant. He was, of course, referring to a certain type of woman, who, in the Germany of the past, would have been disparagingly labeled an Ostblocknutte, an "Eastern Bloc hooker"—a term regrettably still used by some captains to this day. Whenever our flight schedule took us to the corresponding regions, a session with the local prostitutes would be par for the course for some captains. Just like with the stewardesses, you can't tar all the captains with the same brush, but I was struck by how many of them had their own unique customs when taking "shore leave" at night during work trips. One coworker always went to the movies, while another didn't speak to a soul once work had finished for the day, because he would be hunkered down in his hotel room playing video games. But for some of them, flying was as much about brothel visits as lager was about froth or private jets were about champagne.

As we had a large number of Polish clients, we very often found ourselves staying overnight at the Warsaw Marriott. It was a stunning hotel—our favorite place in the city—but many captains were most interested in its bar, which is today still the highest in Europe. It sat at the top of the 460-foot building, providing really phenomenal views. But even more important to the captains, it seemed, was the fact that prostitutes would sit at the bar here and wait for clients. You could soon spot the ladies, or they would make themselves known, by the fact that they would have a full glass of sparkling wine and a dessert in front of them, yet they would touch neither. This wasn't a foolproof system, however, as one of our stewardesses found out when she innocently ordered a sparkling wine and dessert and was promptly approached by a guy who politely but directly tried to find out how much she charged for a night.

Always working, but not always fit for it

The coworker who had this happen to her was my dear friend Yael, whom I'm still in close contact with today. She's followed my entire career, and these days when we have our long evening chats, she's sometimes shocked at how much I've changed over the last ten years. Back then, I was a skinny, friendly, ever-helpful young man—pretty much still a boy—who had only just moved out of home and started to stand on his own two feet. According to Yael, I was much shyer and less confident. She's constantly amazed at how that young man has become the buff, confident dude who loves showing himself off to his followers. Someone who is streetwise and knows how to hold his own at a professional level. (But, for the record, I'm still friendly and helpful.) I find it absolutely fascinating to hear that from someone else, because there was never any specific moment in my life when I decided to change my ways and start living as the Pilot Patrick people know from Instagram and YouTube. It was probably more a case of various developments and changes that made me who I am today. My social media activities have definitely contributed to me continuously working on myself. But I'll go into that in more detail later on.

Yael was also the one who opened my eyes to a quirk of the aviation industry I had never noticed before: Flings between pilots and stewardesses were apparently a daily occurrence. She would constantly rattle off to me who had something going with whom—basically everyone was with someone. I was clearly quite naïve in this respect, because initially, I personally was never aware of any flirtation in the cockpit. But once you're able to read the signs, it often becomes quite obvious. Indeed, affairs between crew members were not a rarity in aviation, no doubt aided by the constricted space of the airplane and the long hours you spend in close proximity to one another. I preferred to keep out of all that. If I'm honest, I didn't find my colleagues' behavior particularly professional, but then again, it was none of my business. I know of a few cases where a pilot and stewardess met at work and are now married. And if a little affair does end up bringing true love, then that's wonderful.

In general, I always liked it when our crew included a stewardess. It usually resulted in me getting on better with the captain because we would have the stewardess as a go-between. If it was just me and a captain, I would sometimes feel a little uncomfortable. It would be subtly conveyed to me that I was a greenhorn who needed to be taught how to be a real man. But I wasn't into dirty jokes or boozy evenings at the hotel bar. When we had a stewardess traveling with us, there was less attention on me, and if we had the night off after just one flight and happened to be in an exciting city, we would often go out for dinner together, and sometimes even party hard.

While I do love a good party, I was never the one pushing for it. That tended to be more common among those who didn't live in Berlin; the ones who, when not working, would sit around in their rural towns going stir-crazy. So, when we were on a trip, they used every opportunity they could to let their hair down. It was actually quite risky, because there was always a chance we would have to be up at the crack of dawn the next morning if a client suddenly decided to charter a flight. Working while bleary-eyed and perhaps even with alcohol still in your system is not pleasant for anyone, but it is of course totally prohibited for pilots. So, I was always very careful not to drink too much. My fears were justified one time in Gdansk when I took a final glance at my cell phone at 4 a.m. We had just gotten back to our hotel after a long night of partying. The stewardess and I were basically sober, but the captain was pretty wasted as he staggered to his room. I was also more than ready to hit the sack, when, just at that moment, a company email came through on my phone. An unexpected booking had been made for 9 a.m. the next morning, so we would need to be ready for work at the airport in less than five hours. It was annoying enough that we had been notified in the middle of the night and only by email; if I hadn't happened to be awake, we wouldn't have known until we woke up the next day, and we definitely wouldn't have made it to the airport on time.

So, in the dead of night, I advised the captain and stewardess. A few hours later, with bloodshot eyes and nowhere near enough sleep, the captain shuffled along to the breakfast buffet. I asked him if he was even in a fit state to fly, and wasn't sure whether to believe his appeasing "I'm fine, all good." Despite the lack of sleep, I personally felt okay, having hardly drunk much the night before. So, if need be, I could have taken charge of the flying and allowed the captain to have a little nap in the cockpit. But this was yet another example of how our company used every chance it could to make a bit of money without so much as consulting those who then had to bear the brunt of these knee-jerk bookings.

These sorts of instances caused us unnecessary stress— after all, we were responsible for getting the plane ready for takeoff on time. Heightened stress levels also increased the likelihood of making a mistake, and that particular flight did indeed result in me having the type of mishap that can end up being pretty costly for the company. I wanted to give the captain a few free minutes to relax, so I took care of refueling. As the gas was being pumped in, there was a catering emergency, so I left the pump running and simultaneously attended to this new task. I then stupidly forgot about the refueling. The filling process unfortunately doesn't stop when the tank is full, resulting in gallons of aircraft fuel gushing out over the tarmac, and the fire brigade having to be called in to "extinguish" it with a big foam blanket. When our company received an invoice from the Gdansk fire brigade for 2,000 euros (about US$2,300) two months later, it was very quick to call me and find out how something like that could have happened.

The whole incident was really a prime example of how things can go wrong: The company slotting in an early-morning job for us in the middle of the night without consulting us, the captain obviously having to fully disclose that he still had alcohol in his system and was not fit for work, and me going along with it all and making mistakes myself. Incidentally, it was understandably awkward for the captain to admit he wasn't in a fit state to fly the plane. Like many other companies, ours also employed freelancers who lived from job to job, and who always feared losing a client if they declined requests.

What we expect from you: Look good

These are all structures and processes you only hope the client doesn't cotton on to. Most industries probably operate differently behind the scenes to how they generally appear on the surface. So, we had to improvise sometimes—whatever! But over time, I did start to notice a pattern of shortcomings. For one, the sales representatives would promise to cater to the clients' every request, without checking whether and how we would actually be able to fulfill these. Then there was the endless cutting of corners. While this may seem like a lucrative way to run a business, we were still providing a luxury product. During the summer in particular, overtime was a daily occurrence, and it was up to us to ensure we got enough downtime. I assume none of you would like the idea of flying in a plane with a bleary-eyed pilot.

And most of you probably expect the flight attendant to know what to do in an emergency. Well, in private aviation, that's not necessarily the case—there are no minimum requirements; they don't even need to complete a first aid course beforehand. Our company was no exception in that it, too, routinely employed stewardesses based on quality criteria that were totally irrelevant to the practicalities of everyday work. I often talked about this with my friend and former coworker, Vivien. She herself had previously flown for a major airline, so was a trained specialist. It also meant she had an expert eye for her untrained colleagues' professional shortcomings. Having a stewardess onboard isn't just about having qualified staff on hand to open "chilled" champagne bottles for passengers. She is also supposed to convey a sense of safety and security. But Vivien says she and her colleagues were ultimately only booked as hostesses. So, our passengers' sense of safety and security was a false one. A training course covering the specific requirements of aviation would also be in the interests of private aviation stewardesses.

Which is why Vivien often talked about a plan that she has now turned into a reality: running training courses for stewardesses. She champions the cause that even small flights should, by law, have a qualified stewardess in attendance. This currently only applies to planes with more than nineteen seats. But even the larger aircraft in the private jet industry usually only have thirteen or fifteen seats, meaning every company can make its own decision as to whether a stewardess works the flight at all, and the criteria for employing her. If you're young and have little ambition but are just looking for a job, you may well find one here. But as a copilot, it always unsettled me when a stewardess didn't know where the emergency exit was or, for example, what to do in the event of an emergency landing.

A few years ago, Vivien founded a company called Fly Exclusive to run training courses for stewardesses. She had a replica private jet cabin built in Berlin-Schönefeld to teach aspiring flight attendants, including those in private aviation, the necessary procedures. Not only do they learn the basics of service, they are also prepared in how to handle emergencies. What do I do if there is smoke or a small fire in the cabin? Where do I find the ax if needed, and how do I use it? How do I pull up the water barrier if the pilot is forced to attempt a landing on water? Vivien is now also in negotiations with the German civil aviation authority (the LBA) in a bid to make her demands heard. The LBA argues, for example, that stewardesses needing to perform safety-related tasks during the flight also require a seat that faces the passenger cabin front-on. The side benches found in most light aircraft do not meet this requirement. But that's essentially a minor problem that could be fixed with a small mirror enabling the stewardess to keep an eye on the cabin at all times. As a pilot, I definitely think it's good that something is finally being done in this area, even though I now fly commercial jets and therefore only work with trained staff.

Cowboys above the clouds

While writing so openly here about my experiences with stewardesses, I should also mention that pilots who have come from private aviation also tend not to have the best of reputations within the industry. I hinted earlier that switching from private providers to the major airlines is not exactly easy. It takes a bunch of ambition and perseverance if you want to take the leap. I wouldn't do without my years as a private pilot, but I'm glad I managed to make the move.

Though we all go through the same training, the large airlines have stricter hierarchies and structures that ensure every team member perfectly knows their place and task area. They're just very different working environments. The constant need for flexibility and the broader task area mean private pilots often just adapt to the requirements. This is a normal process. While there's a lot more improvisation in private aviation, and agreements are frequently very spontaneous, commercial airliners rely much more heavily on regulations. The "privates" are often seen as "cowboys" who find it difficult to stick to the rules in place. The same is incidentally true for pilots who start their career in the German Armed Forces. It was a prejudice that made life quite difficult for me during my shift from private aviation to commercial airliners, but which is certainly not plucked out of thin air. Anyone who has regularly flown on budget carriers will know that, though customers can do whatever they want, they're definitely not king. It's a different story in private aviation, where planes take to the skies on the orders of a single paying guest.

This meant we always had to dance to someone's tune. At the start, I found it fun to prepare for new challenges. While I soon discovered that the job wasn't totally what I had been hoping for, I was willing to buckle down and adapt. I was a newbie who barely knew the industry—so I was aware nobody was going to listen to me tell them how things could be done better. But the fact that there were lots of things that could have been done better was clear, even to me.

The way the Sales department accepted every job without checking whether the promised services could actually be fully provided left us in a pickle on more than one occasion. When we tried to convey to the people in the office that certain things needed to be discussed with us beforehand, it usually fell on deaf ears. It was often as if the non-flying departments were deliberately conspiring to make our lives as difficult as possible as payback for us constantly getting to fly to some of the most beautiful cities in Europe. It even got to the point that I felt certain they were doing it on purpose when we kept being booked into the shabbiest hotels and slapped with flight after flight during the summer months—because the requests would be so last-minute.

I could be going to two different supermarkets on the way to work in the early morning to fulfill an extra client request as cheaply as possible, meticulously preparing the cabin only to then be ignored by grumpy millionaires, scrubbing the onboard toilet because the company wanted to save on cleaners, once again having to miss out on lunch because yet another connecting flight had been booked, or lying on a saggy mattress in a musty hotel room hoping the next day would be less stressful—and the office still seemed to think I was just chilling on a beach in Olbia.

I have never understood the purpose of this "us against you guys" mentality within a company. I thought we should all have been pulling together. Instead, it kept looking as though the Sales department deliberately wanted to make life difficult for us. Coupled with this was the fact that these "ground staff against air crew" tactics didn't exactly create a particular sense of solidarity within our team. The pilots on permanent employment contracts had reservations about the freelancers, and the freelancers understandably acted in their own interests to land as many contracts as possible. After a few initial months of euphoria, I, too, soon realized I was in a pretty conservative industry.

I should have taken more notice during my training. One of my long-established flying instructors was a friendly, laid-back guy who was easy to get along with. I liked him, which is why I was all the more shocked when, one day, he openly and without a trace of irony proclaimed: "Women and blacks have no place in the cockpit." A dumb, ignorant statement that neither I nor my fellow trainees objected to as we should have. For one, he was our instructor—and none of us wanted to rock the boat with him—, and on the other, because he acted so chummy with us. It was a statement that didn't seem to fit my image of him, yet I now see that this view was deeply entrenched in him.

He was not the only one to have this opinion. Many of my colleagues believed that flying planes was a profession that required "real men." The "cowboy aviators" catchphrase has always been nonsense. In the cockpit, it's often about reacting quickly and cleverly—and that doesn't need testosterone-charged chauvinists. But a number of my colleagues didn't seem to share that opinion. I constantly heard them say stupid things about female pilots and stewardesses, and I myself increasingly got the feeling they had their doubts about me. It was nothing to do with my age. While I was the youngest pilot on the team, I was far from the only one under thirty, and would repeatedly hear odd comments even from colleagues who weren't much older than me.

Flying under the radar—but why?

I initially didn't know what was prompting some pilots to adopt an increasingly taunting, and sometimes even subtly hostile, tone toward me. Perhaps, I thought at first, they considered me a try-hard. While they would be putting their feet up before the next flight, I would typically already be in the plane, checking that everything was in order and seeing if anything else needed preparing. I did that because I wanted our clients to have a pleasant flying experience, and I enjoyed creating an exclusive atmosphere. I don't know whether that was why my coworkers felt like they should have been following suit—maybe they thought I wanted to look good and consequently cast them in a bad light. Which was of course total baloney.

At some point, I then began noticing that the comments about me were all of a similar vein; that the other pilots somehow didn't consider me man enough for the job—or at least not the right type of man. That felt particularly strange, because these jibes . . . well, I don't want to say they hit a raw nerve, but, even though they were probably said off-the-cuff and without much thought, they weren't totally inaccurate. I had come to Berlin as a single guy; even during my training, I hadn't had a girlfriend, my third and final relationship finishing at the end of high school. I spent my free weekends exploring Berlin's nightlife, and discovered a world that I had never been exposed to before. Frankfurt's party scene had been pretty tame overall, whereas Berlin had clubs that attracted patrons from all over Europe and even beyond. This open, tolerant culture was much more in line with my personality than the staid, spiritless atmosphere at the company. While I seemed to be breaking the ranks in my job, attracting begrudging looks, I would be breaking out the moves and dancing the night away at the clubs—just doing what I pleased.

I hadn't even been in the city a year when I fell in love again. Though I had previously only ever had girlfriends, Berlin saw me frequently end up at parties that had a predominantly gay crowd. There was not really a specific moment when I made a conscious decision—no "coming out" the way I had seen in movies or heard other people talk about. I can't claim to have had any major moment of realization. I just gradually became aware of the fact that I was at least equally as attracted to men as I was to women, and I didn't see any reason to suppress this. It was that, at one of these parties, I met someone who I found to be exciting, smart, and attractive, and he seemed to feel the same. We partied together, got to know each other better away from the clubs and bars, and, without any kind of existential crisis or self-doubt, one thing led to another until finally it became clear that we belonged together.

We were both from the first generation of young men to have grown up with the Internet. Hollywood movies and pre-prime-time TV shows in Germany had characters who were gay, lesbian, and bisexual. It was very easy for us to come out to each other. I was also open about it to my family and friends, and if the reactions to me now suddenly being in a relationship with a man varied, it was more because some people took a little longer than others to get used to the idea. That's not to say it was a total walk in the park, but friends and family reacted positively, or at least made me feel they respected this change in my life.

It was a different story at the company, where I very deliberately kept this part of my life secret. On the one hand, it just seemed unnecessary to openly discuss my private life in the office or cockpit. Not because it was unpleasant for me, but because I had always felt it a good idea to keep work and life separate. On the other hand, I was already being made to feel out of place, so it definitely wasn't the kind of environment where you'd want to talk about what you did on the weekend with your partner.

Because one thing became very clear to me: If I had mentioned my boyfriend, I would have made myself vulnerable. There was a growing divide between the colleagues who could talk openly about their family, and me, who often felt I had to censor myself so as not to feed the doubts people already had about me. Women were constantly rated on their appearance. This could be in the form of lewd or degrading comments, but were nearly always seeking approval, and would spark further comments. When I was asked whether I found such and such a woman sexy, I could of course answer—just because I was now with a man didn't mean I was blind to the visual charms of the female sex. But I did feel uncomfortable constantly reducing others to their appearance, and I sensed often enough that these questions harbored the suspicion that I wasn't masculine enough to join the conversation. In reality, masculinity can't be all that great if people constantly have to prove it with cheap comments. But I was in my early twenties and in my first job, so I just tried to fly under the radar.

This plan went totally awry when a photo of me started doing the rounds at the company. The organizers of a party had posted some photos, and a female friend had spotted me and linked it to my profile, before sharing the photo on her own timeline. It had been taken at a gay party, hosted by Nina Queer, a tranny known right across Germany. The photo showed me dancing wildly, shirtless. I don't think the female colleague who circulated it had had malicious intentions, but it wasn't long before even my boss had seen the photo. The picture did not bear any references to my job or my employer, but he still found it totally inappropriate. Clients could see it and recognize me, and he could consequently miss out on contracts, he ranted. That was really getting a little far-fetched. In reality, he was the one who had a problem with the photo. What had been a fun, enjoyable night on the dance floor for me was, in his view, an inappropriate display of my sexuality. A sexuality he didn't agree with—and which he believed definitely shouldn't be exhibited in public. Many of my colleagues seemed to share his opinion, even though they themselves were the ones who never missed an opportunity to broadcast their lustful desires to the world.

Goodbye Berlin

I couldn't do much to improve my situation. The photo was out in the world, and that couldn't be undone. I could only hope my boss and colleagues would soon forget the whole matter and just let me do my job. After all, I had been at the company for over three years by then, and my work had rarely given any cause for complaint. I soon came to realize, however, that my boss wasn't going to forget the issue just like that. In the past, we had spoken a few times about me getting promoted. In aviation, that meant switching to a larger plane, that is, completing the necessary type rating to fly a Challenger or even a Gulfstream, which were, in every respect, several degrees better than the Citation XLS I was flying at the time. But, suddenly, there was no further mention of any promotion or type rating. It all seemed to be off the table now.

Instead, I found myself increasingly relegated to stand-by service, and thus prevented from flying. As is the case for any professional pilot, my flying hours were like a currency for me. The more I collected, the quicker I could retrain on larger planes, and the sooner I could qualify for further training to become a captain. My boss was, of course, fully aware of this. So, he punished me by increasingly only rostering me on as a stand-in. The nice guy I had met at the air show a few years earlier, and who had instantly liked me so much that he had given me my first break into a professional career, was now using every opportunity he could to make life difficult for me.

Because he didn't consider my personal and love life appropriate, he clearly felt this was justification enough for his actions. I never introduced him to my boyfriend, nor did I ever talk about my relationship at the company or in the cockpit. That one photo had been enough to turn the vibe against me. A young man simply enjoying his time off by dancing topless at a party obviously aimed at a gay audience. Dirty jokes about women, invasion of our stewardesses' personal space—these were simply trivial offenses in the eyes of the company. But just the thought that I could be "one of those types" had been enough to bench me.

I sometimes had to stick out several consecutive days of 24-hour stand-by, not knowing whether the company would call me at the last minute or not. This wasn't actually allowed, but as I knew it was the company's way of breaking me, I allowed myself to be bullied without really defending myself.

Stand-by service didn't mean getting a call the night before if a colleague went sick. Stand-by service meant I could be called at any time and ordered to be at the airport within sixty minutes. During that time, I would have to get myself ready for work; in other words, jump into my uniform, pack my suitcase, and then drive from my apartment to the airport (which, even when the traffic was good, would take at least twenty-five minutes). So, I always had a packed suitcase at the ready, containing enough stuff to last me a week away if needed. Because when you were called up, you weren't generally told how long you'd be away. It could be a Barcelona return trip, which would only mean about half a day away from home before waiting for the next call. But it could also be an entire week of work, and therefore spending the next five or six nights in hotels.

So, I would sit for days in my apartment, hardly daring to step outside—because Murphy's Law would ensure that an afternoon of exercising or an evening with friends were the exact time I would get a call ordering me to the airport. It was bullying, pure and simple.

At that time, we were all given a BlackBerry to use for communications with the company. The advantage of the Black-Berry was the fact that the data exchanged was encrypted—a feature that other devices like the iPhone didn't yet offer. But we were constantly having problems with the BlackBerrys. For example, they would often switch off after an automatic software update, and then needed to be restarted manually. The company was aware of the fault, but when it happened to me, it was, of course, held against me personally, and I was immediately reprimanded. My BlackBerry had turned itself off one night, so I hadn't realized the company had been trying to contact me in the early hours. After getting up, I first switched on my personal cell phone, which I always turned off at night (the radiation from the BlackBerry was enough). I immediately saw that the company had tried several times to reach me on my personal number. That couldn't be good. I grabbed the BlackBerry—the screen was black. Suddenly, I started feeling a rising sense of despair. I was already out of favor, and this was only going to make things even worse.

The BlackBerry took what seemed like forever to fire up. Then I was finally able to see the missed calls and an email telling me to be at the airport in an hour. The email had been sent an hour and a half prior. I called the company in a panic, explaining the problem, and apologizing to my boss what felt like a thousand times, even though I hadn't been able to do anything about the technical fault; even though I was the one who kept being illegally put on stand-by for days on end. In any case, my call was too late; another colleague had jumped in, and the ship had sailed (or should I say: The plane had taken off). I got the impression my apologies were only digging me further into the doo-doo.

It didn't take long for my punishment to come. OPS contacted me and told me there was a "special duty" for me. Given the way I'd been treated in recent weeks, I could be pretty sure "special" didn't mean an assignment requiring a particularly trustworthy, deserving staff member. The contempt the company had shown for me lately had been too overt for that. The OPS instructions were that I was to go to the airport, collect a package, and take it to Warsaw, where I would hand it over to colleagues who would be waiting for me at the hotel. So, an empty-leg flight. Okay then; that wasn't so bad. At least I would be able to fly again, and no passengers meant no special requests either.

Fat chance! They couldn't provide me with a plane for this, I was told. Instead, I was to take the train. So, I was degraded to a servant, and wasted more than fourteen hours of my life traveling from Berlin to Warsaw and back. The fact that this was really nothing more than trite punitive action became clear to me when I saw the contents of the package. No important documents, no spare parts for one of our planes; just a small espresso machine that could be bought at any appliance store in Warsaw for 99 euros (about US$115). My train ticket alone—coach class, of course—cost 80 euros (about US$93), making it nearly as expensive as the espresso machine itself.

But even after all this, my situation at the company got no better. My boss basically didn't allow me to fly at all. He took obvious pleasure in very deliberately using this as a way of sabotaging my career. I tried to defend myself, but realized I had nothing more to gain at this company. I was sad it had come to this, but also furious at the nasty, intolerant manner in which I was now being treated, despite never having shied away from doing extra work, and repeatedly standing by a company that constantly acted against the interests of its own staff. A company that cut corners wherever it could, and that wasn't exactly professional in its responsibility for its staff's safety. Even if I could have won back the affections of my boss, was I really willing to keep turning a blind eye to all the shortcomings my everyday work would still entail?

The time had come to pull up stakes. I sent off a few applications, and, a little while later, struck it lucky. My new job would take me from Berlin to Hamburg, where I would continue to fly private jets.

That I made the right decision in leaving my first employer was also confirmed to me in retrospect. Former colleagues frequently told me about things that were going on at the company. It even got to the point where the boss eventually had to give the company up after being accused of misappropriating company funds. For example, he kept charging for services that were proven never to have been rendered. He probably assumed (not totally incorrectly) the clients had so much money in their accounts that they wouldn't necessarily notice. (Not that this in any way justifies his actions.) The company still exists, but now has a different owner, and I hope and believe this will be to the advantage of all employees and clients. If my ex-boss has been brought down by his wheeling and dealing, then all I can say is: Karma's a bitch, baby!

There was one positive thing I could take out of the whole thing, and it was the certainty that I had, in principle, chosen the right career. The long weeks where I had been prevented from flying had really gotten me down. Even after four years, every takeoff and every landing still gave me a buzz. Sometimes it's not just a profession; it's a calling.

By the way, the relationship with my partner didn't just survive the job in Berlin; it also survived the years thereafter. He stuck by me during the hard times, giving me advice, and simply being there for me and listening. Our love constantly reminded me that there's more to life than just having a successful job. We're still a couple to this day, and if I haven't ever shouted it from the rooftops in my social media posts, it's because he himself has no interest in being dragged into the public arena. My bad experiences in Berlin are another reason for him not appearing on Instagram and the other platforms. I feel that many of my followers—male and female—like to think I'm single. In this sense, I have to say: Sorry, ladies and gentlemen, but I'm off the market.

CHAPTER

HELLO HAMBURG:
NEW COMPANY, OLD PROBLEMS

So, after four years in Berlin, I was facing the first major change in my professional life. (I didn't have to move for this, by the way; and was very happy about that because, as mentioned earlier, Hamburg and I have never really gotten on.) I realized pretty quickly that it wasn't going to be all sunshine and roses at the Hamburg company either. Some of the problems I had encountered with my first employer appeared to be industry-wide. The new company also scrimped and saved like no tomorrow, and didn't place anywhere near as much emphasis on safety as it should have. To this day, I have never understood that. Very few industries have as clear, elaborate workplace safety regulations as aviation. But it's up to the companies to implement these at all times. It is simply out of order if, in cases of doubt, we pilots and flight attendants are the ones having to ensure our working time is within the legal limits. We are dependent on our employer, so we naturally tend to turn a blind eye and fly another shift, even if it breaches the rules.

Hamburg also had a few of those same types of pilots— boorish dudes with fixed views and outdated mentalities, who considered themselves the epitome of human evolution. This reminds me of one former colleague in particular, who made you wonder how he could ever have been allowed into a cockpit. He was quite an oaf in general—coarse and unkempt—yet never hesitated to hit on the stewardesses, who were all much younger than him. It was sometimes almost tragically touching to watch him fall for these "young chicks," as he called them. He seemed to be totally out of touch with reality. Neither the fact that these attractive, ambitious young women understandably recoiled at his advances, nor the knowledge that he had a wife and three children at home, would stop him from his intrusive infatuations. He looked like a careworn school bus driver from way out yonder; what remained of his thinning hair would usually be sticking out wildly in all directions. Nobody's saying you have to be like the airport in the millionaires' paradise of Olbia and put appearance above all else, but the sight of him certainly caused a few furrowed brows among our clients, accustomed as they were to luxury. Right from the very first glance, he would never look particularly competent, and would do his utmost to reinforce this impression. On more than one occasion, he had been known to go to the wrong airport and wait around cluelessly for his shift to start. I had actually repeatedly heard stories about him even during my time in Berlin. In other words, his reputation preceded him throughout the entire industry. He was considered inept and slovenly, and made no obvious effort to work on this reputation.

When this was coupled with a client to match, it could sometimes have highly unpleasant ramifications. One female client once changed her baby's diaper onboard, and, even though a large trash can had been provided, she somehow managed to squeeze the entire diaper into a small container, barely larger than an ashtray, among the cabin fixtures. The captain didn't appear to have bothered to give the plane an extra clean at the end—even though this was clearly part of his job. The plane, complete with diaper, was then used for another two or three days in hot summer temperatures. While the ventilation system meant the smell wasn't that noticeable when flying, the air would be thick with the stench whenever you entered the plane. It was particularly unpleasant for me when a full flight forced us to seat a passenger on the emergency seat opposite the toilet cubicle.

A client hiding her baby's stinking diapers like an Easter egg, a captain who didn't take his tasks especially seriously in general, "and now, sit back, relax, and enjoy the flight."

It didn't take long for me to get in his bad books. The most important part of the job for him was his after-work beer. And he would become suspicious of anybody who declined to join him. He seemed to take it personally that I didn't generally drink beer. And that was enough for him to question my entire character and, of course, my masculinity. He didn't understand the world anymore, he said to me; but I had honestly never gotten the impression that he understood what was going on in the world ever. After my experiences in Berlin, however, it wasn't a surprise to encounter these sorts of people here again. I was just happy that, as a pilot, I was now experienced enough to know that, if in doubt, I could make up for his shortcomings in the cockpit. Though he had a few decades more professional experience than me, and had made it to the role of captain, I would have otherwise hardly dared be with him in the cockpit. Fortunately, I only ever flew with him twice.

I can understand why many colleagues covered up for him and his constant slackness. The man had three kids, and it didn't look like he would have gotten a job anywhere else if he were fired. But I had now come to realize that this same solidarity among colleagues wouldn't necessarily apply to me. The grumpy old after-work drinker who chased after young women was still more of a "proper" pilot than the young, suspiciously friendly guy who saw women as equals. Plus, aviation is very much about safety, and I believe this is more important than the sense of human sympathy that may have been driving my colleagues to keep silent about him.

Don't get me wrong; I don't believe there are any specific guidelines on what pilots—male or female—should look like. I'm not describing the aforementioned colleague with a view to showing him up. I'm not complaining because I didn't like the way he looked, but rather because he was known for making a lot of mistakes, and because, right from the outset, he didn't care what people thought of him, and therefore of the company. His approach had a negative effect on the whole team. I had hoped the job change would bring me a new, better working environment. But that was only the case to a certain extent, and this particular colleague, in all his regressive glory, was a prime example of what was problematic in the industry.

Female pilots and male flight attendants

If I've so far talked about pilots and captains predominantly being male, and flight attendants predominantly being female, it's because it is still a realistic reflection of the current state of the industry. The gender roles continue to be such that you're most likely to find men in the cockpit and women in the cabin.

I think it's time to break this pattern. I'm for more diversity and tolerance in the industry. If you're a good pilot, then your gender, sexual preferences, or nationality shouldn't come into it. I hope the cockpit chauvinism that so many of my older coworkers have internalized as their male privilege gets sent into retirement along with these very coworkers.

In general, I love working in our industry, and I've met a bunch of great, open-minded people there over the years. It often feels like a big family, and I draw a lot of energy and love from that feeling, which I am then able to channel into my work. But there's still a lingering stench of the "good old days." I, however, won't be forced to adhere to a rigid set of long-outdated ideas. I don't fancy having to listen to stupid comments that I'm not man enough to prove to everyone that I'm the greatest thing since sliced bread. Of course, I can understand that someone thirty years older than me won't really get why I share my life and my love of flying on Instagram. That's a generational thing. But as long as I do my job conscientiously, reliably, and cooperatively, then that's exactly what I want to be measured on: my work. That's the standard I used for all other crew members. Be colorful and eccentric if you want; be what I would consider gray and unobtrusive if it makes you feel better. But if we're going up in the air together, we need to be able to rely on each other—and on the fact that nobody feels treated less favorably because he or she doesn't fit some antiquated view of the world.

Being a pilot or flight attendant is a profession that puts more demands on us than outward appearances would have you believe. Since a crew is a transient kind of team that can change from roster to roster, and from flight to flight, it's all the more important that each of us helps create a friendly, open working environment. "When everyone thinks of themselves, everyone is thought of" is not a motto that will get us very far in our industry.

Last year, a Philippine airline made worldwide headlines for being the first to employ transsexual flight attendants. The American organization NGPA, the National Gay Pilots Association, meanwhile, was founded in Provincetown, Massachusetts, as much as thirty years ago, when a handful of gay men created a place of refuge for gay pilots. No last names were used, and they instead agreed on IDs in order to remain as anonymous as possible in public. These days, the NGPA handles LGBTQ matters worldwide. So, some progress is being made in the industry. Diversity is becoming more visible, and each of us can do our bit to ensure racism, homophobia, and other forms of discrimination toward our fellow people have no place—not in aviation, nor in any other area of society.

FAQ:
What do you pilots actually do?

As a pilot, I've had a lot of strangers and friends ask me the same questions over the years. These questions are often suggestively phrased assumptions that illustrated to me early on that the general public sometimes has a very one-dimensional, but often also quite misguided, concept of what we do. I was repeatedly amazed that many people thought my years as a copilot or first officer—before completing the extra training to become a captain—were simply me being an "assistant pilot." This assumption would make itself crystal clear when someone would make comments like the following about my job: "Ah, you're a copilot. So, you don't actually fly the plane at all yourself. Will you get to at some point?"

You will hopefully still recall that, at the start of this book, I described my first day of work, and how the captain suddenly appointed me to do PF, or "pilot flying." (Anyone who's not "pilot flying," by the way, is—wait for it—PNF, "pilot not flying.") There are always two qualified pilots in the cockpit: the captain and the copilot (a.k.a. first officer). And although it's up to the captain to decide who flies, the copilot obviously also needs to be able to control the plane if the need arises. In any weather, from takeoff to landing. Otherwise I would never have had anything to do for the first eight years of my career. What else would you have expected me to do? Unscrew the thermos for the captain and top up the hazelnut wafers for wealthy patrons?

In general, the PNF is responsible for radio communications and the Operational Flight Plan (OPS). Aside from this, he or she otherwise assists the PF with his or her tasks. There are occasionally situations where a captain is obliged to declare himself or herself the PF—for example, in bad weather or if flying to an airport where landings are particularly challenging.

Another classic preconception I repeatedly encountered was that pilots and flight attendants can just travel the world for free. While there's no doubting we do get around, we generally use the time between landing and departure to just recover a little from the stresses of the last flight. This part of being away can definitely be classified as work. Traveling is a lot different. I absolutely love using my free time to travel, and I do it a lot, as anyone who follows my blog or social media channels will know. But I pay for all these flights myself—and nearly always at full price. The major airlines occasionally offer their staff standby tickets costing only a fraction of the normal fare. But these are seats that are only sold to us at the last minute if the flight is not full. You can't plan your vacation around it. In my time as a private pilot, I certainly never had access to discounted or free tickets. Whenever I went away in my time off, I would still usually wear my uniform; it generally helps you get through security quicker, and the flight attendants sometimes end up giving you a drink or something to eat. On several occasions, I have even been upgraded to Business Class on arrival at the terminal.

Why I don't just constantly fly Business Class anyway also seems to mystify some people. The common assumption is that, as a pilot, I earn a fortune. I can assure you that this is not the case. We definitely can't complain; you can get by very well on a pilot's salary. My gross starting salary at my first job was 3,800 euros (about US$4,500) a month, with more than 1,800 euros (about US$2,100) of this going in taxes and social security payments. That's not a salary that allows you to live high off the hog, especially when you still have loans to pay off from your expensive training. A real perk of the job, however, are the special allowances I get when, for example, I have to spend nights away from my home base (in my case, Berlin). This can noticeably bolster up your salary. I have already mentioned that hotel and food charges are classified as out-of-pocket expenses, and can be billed to the employer. But most employers have tight standard rates for food, meaning you have to pay the difference if you want to have decent meals when away.

The emergence of budget carriers has further shaken up the industry. Customers are able to book flights for a symbolic price of 1 euro (about US$1.20) at any given time, with taxes being added to the total price at the end. Whenever an airline engages in this kind of price dumping, it will inevitably also be reflected in the wages it pays its employees. For us pilots, this sometimes takes on ludicrous proportions. At one point, there was an oversupply of pilots and not enough jobs. And all of a sudden, young pilots who had only recently completed their training were being offered the "pay-to-fly" model, which enabled them to buy their position as a copilot at various airlines. In other words, they weren't paid for their work, but rather had to pay to be able to work. While this didn't allow them to make a living—on the contrary, it only added to their mountain of debt—the airlines' argument was that it enabled them to collect the flying hours they needed to apply for a regular job at the major airlines.

I should mention here that the all-important money issue is different (read: better) for captains. If you do manage to land a job as a captain, your salary can virtually double pretty quickly. At Lufthansa, for example, the starting salary for captains is around 110,000 euros (about US$130,000) gross per year. Of this, a good 50 percent goes in tax, of course, but it still officially puts you among the higher earners.

In addition to a big bank balance, people also always assume I must have perfect eyesight because I'm a pilot. I'm not sure why this misconception is so persistent. In any case, the truth is that you can still be a pilot even if your vision is not perfect. With or without visual aids, your vision must ideally correspond to 20/20 on the Snellen Chart. But there are limits in both directions; for the farsighted, a maximum diopter of +5 is permitted, and for the shortsighted -6. So, bear that in mind before you go buying Grandma Betty with the Coke-bottle glasses flying-lesson vouchers for Christmas.

Incidentally, eyeglasses for pilots are made to particular specifications. They must not press on the nasal bone or temple, because this would restrict the pilot's concentration. The frames must similarly not impede the wearing of head-phones. And the lenses must be curved, so as to cut out potentially distracting diffused light from behind and the side.

Another frequently asked question is: Do airplanes have horns? This is a question that always amused me, because it is both specific and absurd—and because the answer even surprised me. Planes do indeed have horns. But they're not used to shoo other planes out of the left-hand lane when you're attempting a daring overtake maneuver 36,000 feet above the Atlantic. We use the horn to indicate to ground staff that we have an issue. But when the plane's engine is running, it drowns out the signal. The relevant button on the Airbus is known as

"Mechanic Call." The private jet I used to fly didn't have a horn (and that's the reason I've only found out the correct answer to this question in recent years).

Obviously, a lot of people also ask what we pilots do during long-haul flights. Although I—rightly—constantly emphasize the fact that being a pilot is a tiring, stressful profession, I'm not gonna lie; our Autopilot buddy does most of the work once we're up and in the open skies. On short flights of one hour or less, that doesn't mean much, since we're still busy from the very first minute to the last—with takeoff, with reaching cruising altitude, etc. But on longer flights, there are indeed longer phases when there's not much to do. That's when the PNF fills out the flight plan and checks the fuel level, while the PF keeps an eye on the weather along the way and at the destination. Alongside all this, there's also time for other stuff; I write in my logbook, have something to eat and drink, and even sometimes take photos, which I then share with you guys on Instagram.

The longer the flight, however, the more of a strain it can get when you're hunkered down in the very cramped cockpit and don't have much room to move. That's how it was sometimes for me in private aviation when I had to fly longer routes. Even though it theoretically wouldn't have been a problem to leave the captain alone in the cockpit to go and "stretch my legs," there was nowhere I could have gone. The toilet cubicle was at the other end of the plane, and, given our premium clientele, it would naturally have been thoroughly inappropriate to march past them for a quick session on the john.

. . . if you would please excuse me, Mr. Gorbachev

This brings me to another, commonly asked question: Who, of all the famous people I have flown, left the greatest impression on me? Well that would undoubtedly have to be Russian elder statesman Mikhail Sergeyevich Gorbachev. But what in the world does this have to do with having a quick session on the john, so that I would try to segue into it here? I was faced with the exact problem I just described. We were flying the former Soviet leader, who was around eighty at the time, from Geneva to an airport in Moscow. And I was flying with a full bladder.

I've certainly flown a few celebs around Europe, but Gorbachev was a highly impressive guest even for me. After all, this was the man without whom the end of the Cold War, and therefore German reunification, would probably never have happened. We had to be at the airport much earlier than usual. Gorbachev was traveling with three bodyguards, who were painfully meticulous about all aspects of security. Why, on this of all days, I hadn't thought to relieve myself once more before the flight remains a mystery to me. After all, as a private pilot, you're used to the fact that the onboard toilet is reserved for the client, and we had over three hours of flying ahead of us. But quite some time before we entered Moscow air space, I was already feeling the pressure on my bladder. Yet there was nothing I could do; I would have to hold on for a little longer. What felt like an eternity later, with me starting to crumble under the weight of the mental strain, we finally began our approach into the destination airport—and initially weren't granted clearance to land. Dammit! Surely not. But it was winter, so not all available runways could be used, and, Russian practices being as they were, landing slots were assigned somewhat haphazardly. We had to go around. But we weren't cleared for landing on the next approach either, so we flew another loop around, and then another. At European airports, there are at least specific rules on the exact length of the loop you need to fly in such instances, and how long you need to circle for. But the Moscow air safety authorities left us literally hanging in this respect.

We flew holding patterns around the airport for nearly an hour. Below us, the snow was being cleared from one of the runways, yet up in the cockpit, all I could do now was fully concentrate on not peeing myself. I was so focused on holding it in that the captain had now taken charge of radio contact. Behind us sat an increasingly impatient Gorbachev and his bodyguards, while up the front, I was doing the most intense pelvic workout of my life. It was horrendous. We were eventually allowed to make our descent and land. I was not going to be able to last the ten, maybe fifteen, minutes we would have needed for taxiing, parking, and walking to the terminal. No sooner was the plane on the ground and still taxiing down the runway than I jumped out of my pilot's seat, and stumbled into the cabin behind, past Gorbachev and his staff. "Welcome to Moscow, Mr. Gorbachev," I managed to utter, before rushing into the toilet cubicle and closing the door a little too forcefully behind me. After a brief scuffle as I desperately tried to undo my pants, I was finally able to relieve myself.

So much for the question about the most impressive personality I've ever flown. I assume other people who have had the honor of meeting Gorbachev have worthier anecdotes to recount. But I'm not going to lie; my experience always makes for a good party conversation too.

Social media: Where reach isn't measured in tankfuls

All these recurring questions were part of the reason I started keeping an online record of my aviation experiences in the form of a blog in fall 2016. It was my partner's idea. A few months before, I had started sharing photos of my job, in addition to my personal snapshots, on Instagram. You might think that after the episode with the Facebook photo that ultimately led to me giving up my job in Berlin, I would have become warier of social media. But why should I have let that intimidate me? After all, I hadn't done anything wrong. And I kept noticing how much interest my everyday work was generating, even just among my friends. Most people fly so rarely that that in itself is exciting for them. So how must it feel to sit in the cockpit and fly the plane—five to six days a week? Well, that was one of many questions I was able to answer.

At the start, Instagram was simply a way of sharing my everyday life with my various friends, family, and acquaintances. But it was clear that one thing was leading to another.

Through Instagram, I was soon attracting attention from people I had never met. I already had quite a diverse mix of images of my life on there. But I quickly came to realize that the flying-related content was the stuff that had the biggest appeal. I found it inspiring that, with a couple of photos, I was able to share my passion for aviation with people all over the world. This, of course, also meant, however, that I began receiving more and more questions about my work. Soon there were so many that I didn't have time to reply to everyone who wrote to me. So, the blog was the logical extension of my Instagram account. Insta was for the visuals, the blog for the more detailed information.

I would write about my training, my professional career, and generally about the highs and lows of being a pilot. I gradually also started adding lifestyle topics. After all, exercise, a healthy diet, and the many, many trips I did in my time off were also a big part of my life. And my Instagram posts grew more professional too. I suddenly had 5,000 followers, and the numbers kept rising. This gave me the ambition to develop a consistent online presence. I renamed my profile, which was originally *@patrick-berlin*. Now, *@pilotpatric* was born, #notatypo. The *@pilotpatrick* user-name was already taken at the time, which was annoying, because that particular account had no content at all. I wrote to my apparent colleague and namesake, politely asking if he would allow me to use the name, but I received no reply. In the end, I contacted Instagram directly, with no expectation of them being able to assist me further. But, lo and behold, as the other Patrick's profile was empty and obviously hadn't been logged into for some time, Instagram quickly deleted the account so I could take over the name. And that, ladies and gentlemen, was how *@pilotpatrick* was born.

My follower numbers gradually went up. I still remember the first post that suddenly had over 1,000 likes. It was a pretty cool feeling. And the followers kept coming. It took a while to get the first 10,000, but thereafter the increase was pretty constant. At that time, "Instagram influencer" was not yet a title that aspiring teenagers used to crown themselves with simply for accumulating 200 followers, and I sometimes wonder who influenced whom here anyway. What we can assume is that there was some sort of reciprocal effect going on. I was supplying an ever-growing group of people with my aviation-and-lifestyle content, and I absolutely hope and believe that I inspired a few people in very different ways. Whether it was first-hand aviation info or a few tips on a healthy diet or dream destinations, the feedback I got encouraged me to keep going. In this way, Instagram also influenced me, because as I wanted to offer my followers something it meant that these topics also gained importance to me personally.

Traveling had always been one of my passions, but Instagram has enriched my vacations. I do more when I'm away, because it's fun for me to share my experiences. I make the effort to climb a mountain to get that amazing view for my own enjoyment—but it's even more motivating knowing it will also thrill an increasing number of people from all over the world. Exercise and diet have similarly always been important aspects for me, and I take advantage of researching these topics in greater detail, so as to then produce content for my followers. Conversely, I also relish quiet nights at home in my apartment, with my partner, perhaps with a few friends over, even more now.

The fame that can come with social media is a double-edged sword in multiple respects. On the one hand, people with no acting or singing talent see it as a way of achieving a certain degree of publicity, which soon sparks envy in people. (Though the logic behind that seems a little sketchy to me, because all it appears to say is, "They can't act or sing. Hang on, I can't do either of those either! So how come I don't have more followers?") A "friend" actually unfriended me because she found it irritating that I had suddenly achieved a certain amount of fame. She thought she was more deserving of it. At first, she insinuated that I had copied her content, which was baloney. She worked as a stewardess, so there were of course going to be similarities between our posts, but I had never used any of her ideas. When I tried to counter her accusation, the situation only escalated, and I soon realized what her problem actually was. It annoyed me quite a lot at the time, but the more I thought about it, the more I wondered if the friendship had ever been particularly valuable if she was spending the whole time containing her frustration at me having a bigger profile than her.

Focusing on the fact that you don't need to have classic entertaining talents to get a piece of the fame pie on platforms like Instagram leads many people to believe you don't have to be skilled at doing anything at all, but that is, of course, also not true. Yes, I primarily provide insights into my life and job, but this requires more than just a few snapshots with a couple of sentences below them. Considering I mainly run my social media pages as a hobby, I have made them a lot more professional over the last four or five years—and not just in terms of my equipment. I am both the editor and photographer of my own content. I communicate with my followers, which means I also listen to what they're interested in and what not. As companies occasionally ask me to partner with them to promote their products, I have to weigh up which of them fit my image. Because even though authenticity is one of the most important currencies in the world of social media, it's also about having a well-thought-out, consistent image. And you need to make sure you strike the right balance with every new post.

Social media is often slammed for its ability to give any old idiot a platform to build a fan base, which you can then feed with whatever crap comes into your head. You do actually need to have a good sense of the right topics to feature and the right imagery to use. You need to keep your followers engaged, which means making sure you're not constantly repeating yourself. You also want to reach out to new people, so you keep trying new things. And if you want to monetize your social media channels—that is to say, if you hope to get something back for the time, money, and effort you put into them—you need to think even more carefully about how you approach the whole thing. If you want to be in any way professional, I don't think you can avoid advertising.

I myself have often acted as a brand ambassador, though I have always thought through exactly how much the featured product fits me and my image. If you're open to anything, you might fall for anything just as easily. As I don't want to people to think that of me, I will never start advertising sugary sodas or similar products.

Depending on their reach, successful Instagrammers can earn the equivalent of several thousand dollars for just a few promotional posts. But so many factors come into play here that you really can't call it easy money. These sorts of ads need to be positioned and executed strategically; the shots need to be lavish, and you usually have to seek help from people who also need to be paid for their work. Plus, your income is, of course, also subject to tax. Until companies start approaching you, you need to spend a few years working on your channels without any payment. You also need to minimize your promotional posts. If I try to push something to my followers in every second post, it won't be long before they get irritated and unfollow me.

My fans come from all over the world, and they find me in very different ways. Many share my passion for flying, while others are into the lifestyle aspects. My looks—how can I say this without coming across as vain?—are, of course, another reason that has attracted a lot of followers. Anyone who has followed me for a while should have realized by now that this isn't something that totally surprises me, but is instead capital I consciously work with.

I'm passionate about exercise, I'm a fashion enthusiast, and grooming for me has always been more than just a case of "wash & go." If the results of my efforts make me an object of desire for many of my followers, then that's really flattering, and, yes, that is absolutely the intention. It's a great feeling to see a bunch of gushing comments under one of my photos. Interestingly, they are spread pretty equally between men and women, though it's the women who tend to get—I'm trying to be polite and cautious here—more worked up. In general, however, it's all pretty harmless stuff that I can easily live with.

It is not uncommon for my followers to send me gifts either. While these are sometimes just nice little tokens of appreciation, I have also been known to receive jewelry or designer objects that had clearly cost someone a lot of money. (Please, dear readers, don't do this! I know you mean well, but whatever I want, I can buy myself. What I don't want is fans going into overdraft on their account because of me. Save your money or donate it to people worse off than us.)

Unfortunately, there are people who can get quite aggressive in their gushing. Some people forget that there's a relatively clear distinction between social media and real life. I am aware I have made myself a public figure of sorts by sharing so much about myself. But in any commercial business, there's always an area that's off limits to customers. I similarly can't quite understand why some people talk about love and dream of being in a relationship with me. There's a reason social media is called what it is. It's media, meaning content is going to be generated. Pilot Patrick is the content

I create. Of course, it's all focused on me, but it's not a 1:1 representation of my life or personality. And though the way I publicize myself means I lose a certain degree of control over how I'm perceived, it should be pretty obvious that there's not just the pilot; there's also Patrick, the private individual, who exists away from Instagram or anywhere else online.

Over time, I have been repeatedly astonished to find that even people close to me can't quite make this distinction. This is perhaps least surprising in the case of older relatives: They tend to only know social media from what they hear about it, and often don't totally grasp what tempts people to share their lives publicly in this way. I get that; it's part of the general lack of understanding between older and younger generations. Additionally—and this factor definitely cannot be underestimated—career pathways in social media are pretty short if you do it right. My parents' and grandparents' generation had to spend years working hard in order to achieve career success. Instagram et al. might seem like a shortcut, like cheating, to them. Perhaps this book will provide some clarity here. It's certainly been a little more work than just a well-prepared Instagram post.

Even in my circle of friends, there have always been people who suddenly found me arrogant or aloof without anything happening between us in real life. Many appear to have simply scrolled through my feeds on Instagram etc. and then decided the fame had gone to my head without actually talking to me about it. What kind of a friendship is it if you can't even ask me about my motivations directly? I've often gotten the impression that these friends felt I was getting something I didn't deserve—namely, attention. Sure, anyone who poses on the Internet is doing it to attract attention. I'm not going to spend several hours on a photo shoot if I'm then just going to stick the pictures in my diary. And yeah, what I do does take a healthy dose of self-confidence and commitment to a cause. I can understand some people might find this intimidating. But it would have been nice if they had just plucked up the courage to talk to me about it. Nothing has gone to my head. I love my job and my life, and I enjoy sharing it with the world. If others love their job and life, and prefer to keep it to themselves, then that's cool too.

There's work, there's pleasure — and there's Instagram

If Instagram has a relatively young user base compared to Facebook and Twitter, then, as someone over thirty, I must be classified "old." Perhaps this is because a considerable number of my followers are in the forty-plus age bracket. My trip reports are particularly popular among that demographic. I assume these are often people who can only afford to go on vacation once a year, and who get inspiration from me and are able to ease their wanderlust a little. If that's indeed the case, then I'm happy. Traveling is hugely important to me. And I am absolutely aware that it is a privilege to be able to see as much of the world as I do. I'm not one of those people who only care about ticking off as many countries as possible, without really seeing anything of the local culture and nature. I know traveling usually leaves a large carbon footprint, and, as a pilot, I definitely need to be able to take critical questions in this respect. I can hardly exonerate myself here. My job is my job; there is simply no way I, as an individual, can take environmental aspects into account. It's instead about getting the whole industry thinking about how technical innovations and self-imposed restrictions can be used to combat climate change. When it comes to my private trips, I can only say that, as part of the aviation industry, I perhaps just have a very detached view of things. After all, the plane wouldn't be flying without me. Now this may sound a little convenient, and I am ultimately totally in favor of political and economic adjustments being made in aviation to make the industry more sustainable as a whole. But I also know that flying is indispensable. In this modern, globally networked age, and for me personally. So, my simple-minded little reasoning is: Just as there used to be coffee-table books in which people would share tales of their travels to distant lands, there are now bloggers like me. And yeah, maybe it's part of my "influence" to ease other people's itchy feet. Maybe there are fewer trips being taken because people like me enable others to experience our trips in great detail.

Speaking of "allowing people to experience things": I, of course, calculate precisely what I choose to share and disclose about myself on Instagram and other platforms. I cannot, and will not, make anything else public. That's also why I don't reply to personal messages. I find many of these messages nice and touching, and when I get time, I do enjoy reading them. But there are so many that I had to make the decision early on to generally not respond to them if they come from private individuals. I think most of you guys will understand that. If I started answering them all, it would literally be a bottomless pit. There are many followers I can, in good conscience, also call fans; people who build up a rapport with me through social media, and who therefore want more. Sometimes they do this by telling me stuff about their personal life, perhaps expecting some sort of a reaction. But I can't give them that reaction because they're people whose lives I know nothing about. I'm constantly asked the same questions—questions which show that the person only wants to make contact with me in the easiest possible way, be it because they have "fallen in love" with me, or because they think they can benefit from my reach. I've talked about my professional career and my training on my blog, on Instagram, and in YouTube videos. So, when I keep getting private messages asking me how I became a pilot, it highlights to me that the asker hasn't really bothered to get to know me. In general, feel free to send me your nice messages. I'd be particularly pleased to hear if I've been able to inspire you in any way. But please also understand if I don't reply. I hope this book—just like my blog has in the past—satisfies your curiosity and acts as a mini FAQ to give you the info you're looking for.

Although I don't reply to private messages, I don't at all feel that the communications with my followers are unilateral. I read your comments, and follow your reactions very closely—it absolutely enriches my life, and I am happy to reply to comments. That's a public space, which means everyone can read everything when I respond to your questions, requests, and even criticism. I believe it puts the "social" in "social media" when I interact with you guys beyond just posting photos. I sometimes also notice how sad I feel when I don't get reactions. This generally only happens when Instagram or other platforms somehow change the algorithms and my reach gets limited. It genuinely rankles with me when I don't get Likes, even though I know they're a currency whose price is constantly fluctuating. And if I don't post for a few days, for whatever reason, and I hear that my "aviators" have become impatient and are asking where I am, it's a great feeling that totally motivates me.

In any case, my social media presence is more than just a hobby for me. This sometimes makes it stressful, because a well-prepared post can soon end up costing me a few hours. But this investment is worth it. After all, there's no point inviting people to follow my journey only to then keep them locked behind closed doors. At the same time, I, of course, need to make sure I can fully meet the requirements of my job as a pilot at all times. While this can sometimes be a balancing act of sorts, I am, of course, able to separate work from play. I made sure of this right from the outset. There's work, there's pleasure—and there's Instagram.

Fake profiles were an evil I had to learn to live with; random people using my photos and claiming to be me. This can occasionally get really nasty when, for example, someone uses your pictures on dating profiles to attract people, then serves them up some wild stories just to get their money. I have actually had people write to me who swore up and down that I had scammed them. But there were also those who were happy to have found "the original."

There will always be haters and trolls on social media, and they cause trouble on my posts too. I have to admit that, at the start, this got me pretty down. At school, during my training, and even at my first job, I had long been used to almost all my fellow classmates and colleagues only ever reacting positively to me. The circumstances that led me to leave my job in Berlin were the first to put a damper on this, but I knew what had happened there. Yet, I was now suddenly confronted with attacks and accusations I could find no motivating factor for, apart from them simply seeking to be hurtful and invasive, and to cause me personal and professional harm. There is no productive, sensible way of handling such comments except to ignore them and let the positive underlying tone of your own posts speak for itself. At some point, I also came to see that they were nothing more than an unpleasant and actually pretty pathetic expression of jealousy. You mustn't give them the satisfaction of interacting with them. Hence my advice to all users of Instagram and other social media platforms, whether it be because you yourselves are now trying to build a follower base, or because you believe you need to defend me and other Instagrammers: Don't feed the trolls. Every reaction, every reply, is nourishment for these people—and the best thing to do is to cut them dead. Don't engage with them, and instead do what you can to add a whole lot of love and light to the world.

I have a different approach when it comes to criticism from colleagues, which does also happen sometimes. But I've already mentioned that aviation—particularly in the cockpit—is still a pretty conservative industry. So, it's no surprise that there are pilots who find posts and self-expression inappropriate in principle. I can acknowledge and respect this view, but I don't see any reason for them to tell me what I can and can't do. Some also complain that I make it look as though we pilots are rolling in money. Well, as I said, captains' salaries are pretty decent. While we're not talking obscene wealth, you can afford the odd Business Class flight—particularly if you don't have a family to feed. Though I do like to glam things up a little, I don't believe I exaggerate. As such, criticism from colleagues often stems from the simple fact that we have different views of our profession and life in general. That's not a real surprise, and both parties need to be able to handle it—for me, that's the personal criticism, and for my colleagues, that's the fact that I might still just reply with a friendly, "I understand where you're coming from, but have a different view."

I think some of the reservations my colleagues have about me are thus based on the fact that I show aviation as just a normal job. Many are still hung up on the outdated idea that we're gods in uniform who make humankind's long-held dream of flying a reality every day. I don't know whether these are the same people who reminisce about the "good old days" when passengers still clapped upon landing. (I personally am pleased this hardly ever happens anymore.) Being a pilot is certainly not like any other job. I love my profession, and still feel grateful and happy every time I step into the cockpit. But what we do isn't rocket science either, nor is it open-heart surgery. Some in our industry could do well to be a bit more modest. So, just chill, dear colleagues, who think my posts lack substance or dignity. While a landing over spectacular scenery can absolutely spark a sense of majesty inside us, it doesn't necessarily make us kings of the air.

Besides—and this is something I also need to keep reminding myself—we're talking about social media here, where the aim is to create light, positive content. If I complained about the challenges of my work, it wouldn't be long before I'd be flooded with comments telling me how privileged I am. People don't visit my profiles for a deadly serious, humorless portrayal of what it's like to be a pilot. They want to be entertained, and expect me to give them an opportunity to forget their everyday worries for just a few minutes or even seconds. This is another reason why I focus on posts that are funny and mildly informative. I show my "aviators" dream destinations, and provide tips and tricks on areas of life I'm well versed in. If some colleagues think this doesn't meet the standards of our profession, then they're welcome to add their own contribution at any time.

I'm not a daily news broadcast either. I can understand some followers get disappointed when, for example, I don't comment on plane crashes. But I don't know what that would achieve. Information on those kinds of incidents is of public interest, but should be reported by proper journalists. As a pilot, I, of course, follow the debates on air safety issues very closely. But as a self-made social media personality, I don't feel it would be particularly wise to intersperse my dietary tips, travel destinations, and "aviation porn" with my two cents' worth on tragedies, or to discuss disputes between employees and employers within the industry. While I might have an opinion, I don't always have to broadcast it to the world.

My social media presence meant I eventually started getting recognized in public. While at first that was very weird for me, I am now able to appreciate these sorts of encounters as sweet and amusing. It is totally okay for strangers to approach me at any event I'm attending. But when I'm out at a bar with friends—which admittedly hardly ever happens these days—I sometimes have to politely draw a line. This always depends heavily on the individual situation, and when communicated properly, is not a problem for most people. Living in Berlin probably gives me an advantage here, because most Berliners are pointedly casual about interactions with influencers and celebs.

I have, however, also had people suddenly knocking on my door or putting letters in my letterbox asking me for 10,000 euros (about US$12,000). Seriously? Please don't copy them. I love my "aviators," but there is also a line, and those kinds of cases clearly go over it. In general—and I want to reemphasize this—I have a great follower base. When I look at what people do on the Internet, and the kinds of tones adopted in comments sections, I can be truly grateful. The vast majority of my "aviators" are open, sincere, and interested people who are supportive of my journey. I really do get a lot of love, and I think and hope that there's a simple reason for this. These are precisely the values I want to convey in my posts. As Mahatma Gandhi said, "be the change you wish to see in the world."

Spectacular aerobatics

The profile that social media has brought me has incidentally enabled me to enjoy a few experiences I would otherwise probably never have had. In 2017, for example, I was invited to the first ever Red Bull Air Race in the Lusatia region, and was even able to fly with one of the aerobatics pilots—two exciting, action-packed days I will never forget. On the first day, after a brief but restorative sleep at a Dresden hotel, I took a shuttle bus to the EuroSpeedway Lausitz racing circuit in the small municipality of Schipkau. This one-horse town seemed a little out of place on the air race's world-championship calendar, which features the likes of Abu Dhabi, San Diego, Chiba, Budapest, Kazan, Porto, and Indianapolis. Yet, the VIP passes for the Sky Lounge, which were given to me and a few other bloggers, were a promising start. We had a full day's agenda ahead of us. It all kicked off with a hangar tour, where we were able to inspect the aircraft up close. It was during this tour that I met French aerobatics pilot Nicolas Ivanoff, who was a brand ambassador of the watch manufacturer that had invited me to the event.

Clear skies and little wind made for ideal weather conditions, both for the pilots and us spectators. And the Sky Lounge provided us with the perfect view. The tarmac was just in front of our terrace, which meant we had box seats to watch the planes take off and land. Drinks were also provided for us— as well as catering that I nearly missed out on because I was so focused on the aviation spectacle.

These flights were absolutely crazy; I had never experienced anything like it before. The pilots flew at up to 230 m.p.h., subjecting themselves to G-forces of up to 10. G-force is a force per unit mass, which all of you will have experienced yourselves at some point. A roller coaster is a prime example. When the speed abruptly changes as you suddenly head steeply downward, it's the G-force that pushes you back into your seat and makes you feel 200 pounds heavier. The G-force on a roller coaster is probably around 4. The pilots in Lusatia were thus exposing themselves to forces two and a half times that. I tried to imagine how insane that must have felt. Probably pretty awesome.

In actual fact, I would find out myself the next day. The watch manufacturer had organized demo flights with Ivanoff for its guest bloggers. I was stoked. The guy was the best aerobatics pilot in France, and I had admired his breathtaking aeronautical creativity during his race the previous days (in which he was unfortunately beaten by Czech Martin Šonka). He made maneuvers I could only dream of look like child's play. I wasn't at all scared when I got into the Extra 330 LX with Ivanoff. This reassured him too, and I told him he could go through the full repertoire with me. It was a request he was only too keen to fulfill. While he had "fobbed off" the other three bloggers, none of whom had an aviation background, with a standard run (they probably couldn't have been expected to take much more, whereas I already knew a thing or two about flying), he went flat out with me for a full twenty minutes.

The flight experience was incredible; a bunch of adrenalin and even more endorphins shot through my body. I don't want to trivialize your fairground experiences, but comparing this flight with a roller coaster is like comparing a Formula-1 race to a drive in a toy car. Ivanoff had the plane side-rolling (known as barrel rolls) several times, reaching the maximum rolling speed of 400° per second; he flew loops and coasted; he showed me basically all the tricks in the book. It was a phenomenal experience for me, and I felt such a rush that, for a brief moment, I actually lost consciousness. But I had never felt so happy. (You can see a short video of it on YouTube; just search for "Pilot Patrick on his first aerobatic flight." I almost think that that one minute describes the experience better than my words ever could.)

I had a similar experience (another opportunity I would never have had if it hadn't been for my social media presence) a good year later when another Swiss watch manufacturer invited me on an aerobatics flight. This time, I headed to the eastern French city of Dijon, which is to mustard what champagne is to sparkling wine. The jet team that had invited me is the world's largest civil jet acrobatics team. Incidentally, you can't buy this kind of experience; you're either invited or you're not. On this occasion, we would be flying in an Aerosol L-39 Albatros, a training aircraft for fighter pilots. And just as it had done the previous year in Lusatia, the weather came to the party again: Clear skies and a sunny 71 degrees. But before getting into the Albatros, I was introduced to an old dame: the Bücker. She had been around for eighty-five years, but she was magnificent and had been kept in immaculate condition. These types of aircraft had been used during World War II to prepare the *Wehrmacht*'s fighter pilots for their missions in the Messerschmitt Bf 109. (So, similar to Aunt Ju, a pretty grim history, but you can't really blame the aircraft; they're still marvels of engineering for their time.) The Bücker continues to have an excellent reputation among pilots to this day, because it is so smooth to fly and responds particularly well to commands. I then flew with Guillaume, one of the pilots who was hosting me that day, over the stunning landscapes of Dijon and surrounds. And Guillaume was still able to get a few acrobatic stunts out of the old dame, despite her eighty-five years.

This was followed by the safety instructions for the flight in an L-39 Albatros. The emergency exits were far from being to my left and right. In the worst-case scenario, the pilot would call "Eject! Eject! Eject!" to signal use of the ejection seat, which meant initiating an evacuation by pulling the red lever between your legs upward. This would eject you and your seat from the plane, before a parachute opened up to enable you to glide safely back to earth. If this were conventional practice in commercial airlines, I'm sure a few of you would never set foot in a plane again.

This time, we flew in a four-jet formation; I sat in Jet Number 3 with my pilot Doukey. Doukey used to be a fighter pilot in the French army—so I could be sure he had a few tricks up his sleeve that would impress me. I actually still get goose bumps just thinking about the takeoff. We were barely airborne and were already flying in formation. It's an insane feeling to suddenly be up and flying so close to other planes. It almost made me feel a little queasy, but within seconds I could see how confidently Guillaume, Doukey, and the others controlled their aircraft. This was precision work like no other, yet they made it look effortless. There were times when we were flying just ten feet apart at speeds of 435 m.p.h. Barrel rolls, loops, and even upside-down maneuvers were again part of the repertoire. It took my breath away. What an experience!

Doukey then left the formation and fulfilled a wish I hadn't even dared to express. "Now you take over the controls," he said. "Are you serious?" I asked, somewhat incredulous. "Sure!" he grinned. Utterly invigorated by this rush of speed, I did two barrel rolls, before rejoining the formation. He again handed the controls over to me for the landing approach, and I did a circuit of the aerodrome at a speed of 155 m.p.h. It felt as if I had gone from a Fiat to a Mustang, but I knew I could have total confidence in my piloting skills. At no point was I scared of losing control of the aircraft, but Doukey took charge again for the landing itself. Even hours later, when the flight had long ended, I was still grinning from ear to ear. One of my aviation dreams had come true that day. If it hadn't been for the watch manufacturer inviting me after coming across my blog and Instagram, none of it would ever have happened.

Another real highlight was my vacation in Dubai—which was paid for entirely by the Emirati city. With flights, accommodation, and the activities offered to me, the whole trip would definitely have been worth close to US$20,000. I myself wouldn't have been able to afford it, but a local marketing firm working on behalf of the city wanted to use my reach to attract more tourists. There's no question that a large follower base strokes one's ego, but it does also have a certain market value.

No photos, please!

Among the people pretty critical of my social media presence right from the outset was, unfortunately, my Hamburg-based employer at the time. I, of course, always made sure none of my channels ever named the company I worked for. And at no point did my social media activities affect my work performance in any way. Yet I was told the company could lose customers if employees posed in front of or inside any of its fleet. This was compounded by the fact that a few stewardesses had gone completely overboard and had had photos taken of themselves lounging in our planes' luxury seats and drinking champagne. I could well understand how those sorts of actions would upset the company management. What I didn't get was this: If my boss could see how a bad picture could cast the company in a poor light, why couldn't he also see that the opposite was also true? A couple of well-placed pictures could have helped the company cultivate an open, contemporary, sophisticated image. My content at the time was also heavily focused on my job as a pilot. I showed people a side of flying they otherwise might never have seen. The company could have used my expertise and maybe even unlocked a completely new client base.

But just as many of our clients and pilots were conservative, so too was my boss, who actually wanted to ban this new-fangled gimmick called "social media." As I had the greatest reach of all his employees, I was obviously a particular thorn in his side. Instead of seeing the potential my skills could have offered his company, he asked me to completely stop my Instagram activities. And he wasn't just worried that his company's good reputation could be harmed by me posting about my job and aviation in general. The fact that I made sure never to identify my employer wasn't enough for him. Clients, he feared, could still somehow figure out what I was doing online, and choose to book their flights elsewhere. (Why would they have done that?) My followers could somehow find out where I worked, and that could harm the company, he said. (What was the link there?) I, of course, understood he was entitled to limit my content in every respect that directly affected him and his company. But in no way did he have the right to prohibit my social media activities in general, and on this I insisted.

Similar to what had happened with my Berlin employer, the company started to make life difficult for me. I had now been a pilot for a good six years, and was still flying a Citation XLS.

Once again, despite agreements to the contrary, the prospect of a promotion in the form of a new type rating seemed to have evaporated. I'm quite an ambitious person, and I found it painful and unreasonable to be thwarted in this way. The company management's short-sightedness here was highlighted to me by various enquiries from potential clients who found me through my social media channels. I had now built a substantial reach, and people were approaching me directly to book me as a pilot. I could, of course, have forwarded these enquiries to my employer. In other words, my Instagram presence would have given him a monetary advantage, as I had repeatedly tried to tell him. But I was always met with a stubborn rejection, and so had little motivation to help the company out beyond my rostered jobs.

Just as had happened a few years prior in Berlin, the whole thing ended up getting to a stage where it diminished my enjoyment of the job. At one point, the prospect of a promotion resurfaced, but I could only have this if I were willing to forego the associated pay rise. In other words, more responsibility for the same salary, at a company that charged the equivalent of ten thousand dollars for a single flight! I knew there was nothing more for me here. So, I once again started looking around the job market. I yearned to find an employer who abided by wage agreements and safety requirements, and didn't worry about which social media I used in my free time. The time had come to turn my back on private aviation. (My Hamburg employer has now incidentally banned all employees from posting on social media.)

CHAPTER

GOING UP A SIZE

My new job took me far away from filthy rich clients with absurd special requests, and far away from the petty austerity measures of an employer that puts up a ritzy façade but is too stingy to invest in a solid foundation. I could finally switch to a larger aircraft: In future, I would be flying an Airbus A300. What a difference from the Citation XLS! At nearly 150 feet wide, the Airbus had more than three times the wingspan of the Citation, and, at 177 feet, was four times as long. Fortunately, I didn't have to pay for the type rating this time; it was covered by my new employer. Some intense training in the simulator was followed by a few takeoffs and landings using the "touch-and-go" method. As deceptively realistic as simulator "flying" may be, the first time I got airborne in the Airbus was an overwhelming, goose bumps-inducing moment. I was then able to apply to the LBA, Germany's civil aviation authority, for the license entry of the A300. While waiting for my updated pilot licenses, I was permitted to fly in the cockpit a few times as an "observer." Once I received my license back, it was then time for the "line training," which began in March 2017. This meant that, for the first eighty flights, a duly trained pilot had to supervise me.

It was actually reassuring to have this supervision, because switching from a private jet to an Airbus was no mean feat. I had accrued 2,500 flying hours in my career to date, yet nearly everything was suddenly new again. For eighty entire flights, all of my actions in the cockpit were observed and assessed at a subsequent debriefing. The captain gave me a detailed account of his experiences with the aircraft, and pointed out peculiarities I needed to remember. I had to memorize the operation manual, and also had to learn the company's standard procedures. Two flights then ended up being a final examination of sorts. I flew one of these as "pilot non-flying," and the other as "pilot flying." The final assessment contained a brief written summary of my performance in handwritten capital letters: "Mr. Biedenkapp did an excellent job during the line check. He followed our standard procedures excellently. He has a positive attitude and is very motivated. It's great to have you part of our team now. Well done!" It read a little like a first-grader's school report, but it still put a big smile on my face.

Not only does the Airbus have more system displays than the Citation; its controls are also much more sensitive. Even my first one hundred hours of flying brought me a few impressive experiences: a storm, complete with lightning flashes right in front of our cockpit window; a landing with strong crosswinds, which was fortunately less challenging than it would have been in the much lighter Citation (less surprising when you compare the numbers: The Airbus, at 97.5 tons, was nearly eighteen times heavier than the Citation); and I even got to see a St. Elmo's fire—a rare weather phenomenon in which luminous plasma is created by electric charges.

Private jets or commercial airliners? Both have their advantages

Ultimately, you don't need much more than a good dose of adaptability and team spirit to adjust to working conditions at a major airline as an experienced pilot. I didn't find the transition difficult, but I was also still quite young when, at twenty-seven, I was fortunate to be able to make the switch. In general, there is one particularly stubborn preconception: That private pilots are mainly those who couldn't make it at the major airlines. That's a generalization and pretty much baloney. The different ways these two sectors operate is in fact one of the reasons why some pilots find one type of employer's working conditions better, while others will feel more comfortable with the other type of employer. As a young person, I enjoyed private aviation specifically because it was very unpredictable and therefore exciting. Now, in my early thirties, I appreciate the safety and fixed procedures in place at my commercial airliner job.

I definitely had a few curious creatures during my first years as a pilot—and I'm talking about the passengers; not the planes. While this could be incredibly annoying, it was also exciting, funny, and thrilling at least equally as often. Sometimes even glamorous. As a private pilot, I had been able to choose my own home base. I spent a while living in Barcelona, operating flights out of there. But most of the time, my home base was Berlin, and I would fly from Tegel or Schönefeld airports to Nice, London, or Paris. We would often have to fly to work as passengers on commercial flights if, for example, the plane was in Warsaw and our duty started there. These days, if a flight I'm operating doesn't start in Berlin, I use my employer's flight network to get to the relevant airport. This is both practical and annoying, because it means I miss out on all the air miles I had previously been able to accrue flying with other airlines. (I incidentally also no longer own a car. Both as a private pilot and now in my current job, I spend at least half the month away from Berlin. And when I am in town, car-sharing services are more than adequate for me to get from home to the airport.)

Ever since I have started flying for a commercial airline, I have been receiving my roster a month in advance, which enables me to plan my time off. In private aviation, on the other hand, we were basically just on call. This could be exciting, and it was thanks to our clientele that, exceptionally often, we were able to get to some of the most vibrant and beautiful cities in Europe—cities where the jet set would flock, where prominent political and business figures would hang out. But the flights themselves were often too short. It was not uncommon for a working day to simply consist of a 60-minute flight, while the rest of the day was spent preparing the plane, attending to catering, serving our clients, keeping them happy, cleaning the plane, finding a hotel for the night, and finding out what the next day would bring. In six years as a private pilot, I accrued 2,500 flying hours. Based on 220 working days of eight hours a day in a year, that equates to 10,560 working hours over this six-year period. And that's not even counting overtime. As such, I didn't even spend 25 percent of my working time flying.

Yet, I was constantly on call, and that wears you out in the long run. Now, sometimes the constant uncertainty did indeed make for some cool moments. One time, I said to my colleague that I really felt like flying to Mallorca or Ibiza. Barely two hours later, a new order came in: first to Mallorca, then to Ibiza. But these instances were, of course, the absolute exception. In most cases, the uncertainty, the endless waiting around, and constantly being on call was just stressful.

Very, very few pilots spend the majority of their working time flying. Anyone flying for a budget carrier will accrue up to 900 flying hours a year, which—again based on 220 working days a year—still only makes up half the working time. (This might sound relaxing, but it is the exact opposite.) In my last three years as a pilot for a commercial airline, I have accrued an average of 450 flying hours a year. I fly no more than three routes a day, and the procedures are much more relaxed. In private aviation, I was usually at the airport two hours before departure, whereas now—like all other crew members—I only get there an hour before the first departure. And once the last flight is done, I don't have to then scrub the onboard toilet; I can leave the plane within about fifteen minutes.

When I used to get to work in the morning, I often wouldn't know where I would end up by the evening. For our crew, that meant not being able to book a hotel before getting the okay from the company. Then, however, we could choose our own hotel. (There were, of course, financial rules we had to follow.) I had a passion and knack for choosing hotels, which is why my colleagues usually left that job to me. But that also took up a lot of my time, and, as we always had to book exceptionally last minute, we could only hope the hotels had enough rooms available. With my current roster, I would be able to plan in advance, but the company takes care of booking accommodation when we have to spend nights away from our home base.

I don't fly to as many different airports now either. After 200 flying hours with my new employer, I had covered virtually our entire route network. In this respect, my work has become more manageable, but it also means I no longer fly to some of my favorite airports.

Private aviation had a few perks I've had to forego. On most flights, for example, there would be a lot of catering left over, which my colleagues and I were allowed to eat. And it wasn't just Milky Ways; depending on the client, it could often be real delicacies. Most of the private terminals would also have a lounge area for crew members, meaning we could enjoy a bit of comfort between flights that is not offered at the terminals I now fly to.

The bottom line is this: My years as a private pilot were an important, educational time in my professional career. I wouldn't do without them, and I can imagine that this sector of the aviation industry would be the right long-term choice for many pilots. At this stage of my life, I personally find working for a commercial airliner more relaxing, while still providing me with enough variety. It is more "grown-up" work overall, which better meets my needs at present. The relatively high degree of roster reliability means I also have enough time to dedicate to my social media channels, which I now spend much of my spare time on. Flying is my passion—a passion that remains as fervent as it was on the very first day. But the contact with my "aviators" has become hugely important to me in recent years. Instagram and YouTube in particular are platforms that allow me to give free rein to my creativity— a great way to counterbalance my work, where I always have to keep a cool head. But I don't want to discount a return to private aviation. It's certainly possible I might feel like going back to it at some point.

Switching to the left-hand seat, or: My rise to captain

After eighteen months in my new job, I applied for a captain's position within the company in the summer of 2018. I knew I would be getting myself into a tedious process that would take months. These application processes consist of many different phases, and are unavoidable if you want to "sit on the left-hand side" of the cockpit, in other words, the traditional captain's seat. Not only do you need to meet all the legal criteria; you also have to prove you have the right attitude and personality to fulfill the requirements that come with a captain's position.

The specific requirements can vary from company to company. But the minimum requirement is of course to hold a full ("frozen"), valid ATPL. (Okay, okay. I'm not going to pretend to expect you to have learned all the abbreviations mentioned so far in the book by heart. ATPL stands for Air Transport Pilot License here.) And you need to have recorded a sufficient number of flying hours. At some companies, that's 1,500, though this is the absolute minimum. Most require 3,000 hours or more. You also need to undergo countless simulator sessions, training courses, and other aptitude tests.

I had long pursued the aim of becoming a captain before my 30th birthday. When I moved from private aviation to commercial airliners, I had basically already given up on that goal. Both of my previous employers had thwarted me for petty, trivial reasons, and denied me promotions I was actually entitled to. I would, of course, first have to prove myself to my new employer before being considered for any kind of promotion, leave alone to the role of captain. But when I saw the job advertisement, I immediately decided to try my luck. If I was actually successful, I would still be able to achieve my goal. If not, at least I had shown ambition and would improve my chances for future job vacancies.

The application was in the form of a digital questionnaire. In response to the question of why I was applying for the role, I wrote: "Two years ago, I was offered the role of captain at a private jet company. That had always been my goal. Nevertheless, I decided at the time to turn my back on business aviation in order to tackle new professional challenges as a pilot of a wide-bodied aircraft with a completely different set of operations. Even if it meant I would have to keep being a first officer. Now I meet almost all the requirements to qualify for the position of captain advertised here. With long-time professional experience, I am now prepared and willing to take on responsibility for safe procedures and the entire crew."

And when it came to the question of why I considered my-self a suitable candidate, my response included the comment that "I would describe myself as a very positive person who loves sharing his passion with others. This contributes to a pleasant working environment in the cockpit. As a captain, I would continue to represent the company just as I have always done. I am willing to take on new professional challenges and more responsibility."

The HR department asked captains and the company management if my application should be taken into consid-eration or not. I was soon given the green light. I had made it to the next round. This was swiftly followed by a one-hour flight in the simulator, including takeoff and landing, as well as some (simulated) operational problems. Two instructors helped and supervised me here; one operated the simulator, while the other sat next to me in the captain's seat. It was once again less about evaluating my flying and more about assessing my flight-management and decision-making skills. I acted in my usual role of first officer, except that I received no help from the captain to my left when it came to any attempts at problem-solving. At first, I was nervous, excited, and happy—all at the same time. But, once seated in the simulator for the first time, I took a deep breath and concen-trated on proving my knowledge and skills. I was then asked a few questions about operational procedures and technical aspects. I went home with mixed feelings. It would be a while before I received my results.

The day finally came in early 2019; I had officially qualified for further training as a captain, after which—if I were successful—I would be promoted. But first there were training courses, simulator flights, line training, and various check-ups. Nevertheless, I had taken a giant leap toward achieving my dream. If everything went smoothly, I would be the captain of a major global airline in May—before my 30th birthday. But nothing was guaranteed yet, because the advanced training courses would only go ahead if enough participants had been found—and, at that stage, I wouldn't have been indispensable to the company.

Captain's training

During those weeks of waiting, I continued to fly the A300 as first officer. But my time on the right-hand side of the cockpit came to an end faster than I expected it to. On January 31, after eight long years, I completed my final flight as first officer—to sunny Tel Aviv. This was followed by a seamless transition to the start of UTC training in early February. (In this case, UTC didn't stand for Coordinated Universal Time, but rather "upgrade to commander.") It kicked off with a one-week basic course, after which I was officially no longer allowed to fly as first officer. There were six other participants completing the course with me. I had expected to be the youngest, but there were actually two aspiring captains who were younger than me, though that wouldn't take away from my ambition. If I achieved my goal and officially got to wear the four stripes on my uniform before I turned 30, I would be happy.

Just to digress real quick: The uniform stripes, of course, mean something. While there is no standard rule across all airlines, four stripes generally indicate a captain ("Pilot in Command")—the person who has the say onboard. All other crew members are subordinate to him/her, and are obliged to follow his/her instructions. I myself had so far been flying with three stripes, denoting my rank of first officer. Some airlines have a system in which one of the three stripes is broader, indicating that the person has more experience than others within their rank. Juniors sometimes also only have two stripes, flying officially as second officer. Phew, I think that adequately describes the system. Uniform stripes are also used in seafaring to highlight rank. As you can imagine, the whole thing dates back to military and naval ranks.

The content of the basic course focused on the following areas: law and regulations; responsibility and leadership qualities; operational procedures; CRM (Crew Resource Management); and LVP (Low Visibility Procedures). The captain of an airplane not only bears responsibility for the crew, but also for all passengers and cargo. CRM plays a similarly important role in air safety. It includes teaching practical, nontechnical skills designed to enable crew to clearly communicate, in exceptional circumstances, who is responsible for which tasks, and how these tasks are to be performed. The command "All hands on deck!" describes a situation in which the help of all those present is needed to achieve an objective, and CRM is basically like an order for coordinated implementation of this call. The idea here is to prevent "human error" or counter its effects. LVP, meanwhile, particularly involves procedural instructions for taking off and landing in bad weather with limited visibility.

This basic course was then backed up the following week by simulator training—in Berlin, which was of course great for me. I prepared myself thoroughly in order to prove to my trainer and myself that I was a suitable candidate to fill the left-hand seat of the cockpit. This section of the training consisted of six simulator sessions and a final test. Each of the six sessions was dedicated to a particular training requirement. Focus areas included procedures in the event of engine failure or fires, as well as practical implementation of LVP. These training units in turn collectively constituted practical implementation of CRM, because they revolved around the nontechnical aspects of flying, and the captain's associated responsibilities. Nontechnical tasks are all those relating to flight management, which is part of the captain's role in every flight. He/she assigns tasks and prioritizes them, or he/she makes all decisions and communicates these to the subordinate crew.

Among the things I found difficult was the move from right to left. All the knobs and levers were now on the opposite side, and my brain had to rewire everything it had stored up over the years. To a lesser extent, many of you have probably already experienced this for yourselves, if, for example, you're a German or American who goes on vacation to England: You suddenly have to first look right, then left, before crossing the street. And if you've ever gotten into a car and suddenly had to change gears using your left hand, you'll probably have a better understanding of how confusing this switch can be.

I also learned many flying maneuvers and SOPs (Standard Operating Procedures) that were new to me, such as rejected takeoffs and engine fires involving evacuation of the aircraft on the ground. Aviation has a comprehensive V-index, where "V" stands for "velocity," and a rejected takeoff can only happen at minimal speed, that is, up to V1. If the plane is already moving at a higher speed, normal takeoff needs to occur, as the tarmac will not be long enough to brake. In the event of an engine fire, there are two checklists the captain has to work through in a structured, coordinated manner; it is ultimately also him/her who decides whether the plane needs to be evacuated or not.

Each of these six training units took six hours: a one-hour introduction, four hours in the simulator, and a one-hour assessment. This was then followed by my check flight in the simulator in late February, which I completed together with a first officer who had just finished his training. This enabled me to actually prove I had fully mastered the requirements of a captain, because my sidekick, as a newbie to the profession, had to be able to rely entirely on my knowledge.

This check flight completed the qualification and testing component of my captain's training. Now came the bureaucratic component in which the LBA (Germany's civil aviation authority) had to upgrade my CPL (Commercial Pilot License) or "frozen" ATPL to a full ATPL so I could officially fly as a captain. But even that wasn't the end of the promotion process: Though I could already call myself a captain with the "unfrozen" ATPL, I was still flying with only three, rather than four, stripes. I had to fly the first twenty-five flights in my new role under supervision. This is known as "line training," which is kind of like an orientation to complete the promotion process. Sitting to my right here was not a first officer, but rather a training captain.

The line training took place as part of regular flight operations onboard an A300. I had to familiarize myself with the procedures and new challenges, and the accompanying captain would intervene whenever necessary with tips and corrections, while simultaneously performing the role of first officer. But all the captain's tasks were generally left to me, meaning I had to instruct both him and the crew.

The key points of this phase were:
- internalizing actions for flying on the left-hand side of the cockpit;
- familiarizing myself with all of the captain's task areas;
- reviewing and furthering technical knowledge and operational procedures;
- simulating approaches and landings with poor visibility; and
- consolidating nontechnical skills such as management, decision-making, and communication.

I would love to say everything went smoothly right from the start, but I was, of course, still pretty unsure and nervous, and this repeatedly became apparent. For landing approaches in particular, the altered view you have from the left-hand seat is quite a challenge. I found it difficult to focus precisely on the runway's middle line. This is important, because you need enough leeway on both sides in the event wind gusts or technical problems push the plane to the side. After four attempts, however, my landings were largely accurate again. I had spent eight years controlling the yoke with my right hand and the thrust with my left. This was now suddenly inverted, and once again had to be internalized. But I managed to do this relatively quickly, and, after a few flights, I already felt comfortable in my new role as captain.

The line training concluded with my first real flight alongside a first officer. The instructor was now sitting in the observer seat behind us, observing us, but would only step in if absolutely necessary. He didn't have to. To my great relief, everything went smoothly. I remained confident and relatively relaxed from preparation, to takeoff, to landing, and was thus able to put my knowledge, skills, and leadership qualities to the test. My training captain offered me his congratulations in a very simple, no-fuss manner after landing. I had passed, he told me, and praised me on my excellent performance. There may not have been any confetti or brass band, but, at that moment, I felt insanely happy—and rightly pretty proud of myself.

What would change now? A coworker summed it up for me: "You're now the conductor of an orchestra," he explained.

"You delegate and set the tone." As a captain, I would not only be instructing the crew; I would also be managing all in-flight procedures, such as communicating with ground staff and keeping to flight times. I would now be keeping an eagle eye on everything at all times, and analyzing new information— so-called "situation awareness." I would then delegate the necessary resulting actions and communicate these to the relevant crew members.

Put simply: I was in total control.

Forever on solid ground? Coronavirus (COVID-19) and its consequences for the aviation industry

I'm writing this in July 2020. For nearly four months now, most of the aviation industry has been at a standstill. The reason? Coronavirus—SARS-CoV-2, to be exact—, which emerged in China's Wuhan province in late 2019 and spread all over the world. As the virus can spread particularly easily when many people come together in confined spaces, but also because many countries have imposed extensive travel bans, most planes have been grounded ever since the WHO declared the coronavirus a pandemic on March 11, 2020.

The consequences of this pandemic have been devastating for a number of economic sectors. Restaurants had to close for months, retail suffered severe revenue losses, and long nights of clubbing and concerts continue to be prohibited. But few industries have been hit as hard as aviation. We still don't know when anything resembling normal operations will resume. Indeed, we can't even be sure we'll ever be able to return to a situation comparable to pre-COVID times. It is much more likely that the entire industry will have to be restructured and rethought through over the long term.

Most planes are currently parked on unused runways. According to the European Organization for the Safety of Air Navigation (Eurocontrol), aviation in Europe has plummeted by 90 percent when you compare the figures for April 2019 and April 2020. Lufthansa, Germany's national carrier, completely ceased operations of its subsidiary Germanwings back in April as part of the COVID-induced economic crisis. Other European airlines will also disappear off the radar forever. And it's not just pilots and flight attendants who have been forced to stay home. Most ground staff have no work until further notice. The closely related tourism industry—the main source of income for many countries around the world— has of course also been largely paralyzed.

Countless hotels, guesthouses, and restaurants that live off international visitors will have to shut over the short or long term due to lost earnings. The aviation industry is the central hub of a giant, complex economic system that is on the verge of collapse. Obviously, there are heated debates over the extent to which the preventive measures taken worldwide are appropriate to the situation. It's a difficult issue causing clashes between various sectors, such as industry, politics, and medicine, without anyone, even within their own sector, being able to agree on a clear approach (which is partly also due to the fact that the situation is changing daily). On the one hand, the economy needs to be gradually restarted, and on the other, virologists fear a second, and maybe even a third, wave of the pandemic. Every country has adopted its own policy in this respect—and this is sensible, considering how different each one's situation is. European, or even world-wide, standards that are extraordinarily important for the aviation industry may be a thing of the past for the foresee-able future.

The global airports association ACI is endeavoring to establish new regulations applicable internationally, or at least to all European airports, to enable controlled, albeit limited, operations. The sheer volume of parties that need to be involved here makes this incredibly complex. So, some heavy turbulence in an industry on which many millions of jobs depend—directly or indirectly—worldwide.

Nobody foresaw the fierce impact the pandemic has ended up having on the aviation industry. That may have been naïve, because scientists have long stated that a global pandemic was not a question of "if," but rather "when." Yet, nobody, anywhere, was prepared for this scenario. Even in very well-positioned industrial nations, there was a lack of available intensive-care beds and ventilators. Businesses, schools, universities, and other public institutions had few crisis plans to fall back on.

Germany took comprehensive measures to contain the infection relatively early on. Compared to countries like Italy and the United States, which were hit massively hard by the coronavirus, the number of infections and, in particular, deaths here has so far been much less dramatic. There continues to be public discussion over whether the lockdown was necessary in the extent that it was implemented. I'm not a doctor, virologist, or politician, and when I say here that I believe we could have fought the virus with restrictions that would have had less drastic impacts on the economy, that's just my personal view. But the collapse of the aviation industry is something that hits close to home. Aviation has been a lifelong passion for me, and I want the situation to restabilize as quickly as possible. I suspect this will take around two or three years, and nobody can say yet what the "new normal" that we will hopefully have reached by then will look like.

You often hear people talking these days about how the impacts of the pandemic have had a positive effect on the environment, and this is of course true. Aviation's carbon footprint is not insignificant, and if the current situation has highlighted to us that many of the flights we take are avoidable, then perhaps that will be a long-term gain. But the complete halting of a vast and far-reaching economic sector has devastating consequences of a different kind, and it will cause considerable harm to countless lives.

We need to talk about how we will revive the industry, how we can save airlines from collapse, and how we can act responsibly, but also profitably, under the new conditions. We also need to talk about how we can make aviation more sustainable and eco-friendlier overall. If we want to take any positives from the present situation, it should be that we focus much more on sustainability as we restart the economy. Flights for less than 10 euros (about US$12) and commuter flights between cities like Berlin and Frankfurt were already irresponsible before the pandemic, and it would be good to abolish these in future. But it is also true that we live in an age of globalization, and, without aviation, it cannot function.

A plane ticket should not cost less than a train ticket, but price shouldn't be the only factor either. There also needs to be better rail networks and faster connections, if train travel is to be made more attractive. We might even be able to completely do away with some flights. We should all ask ourselves how many vacations we really need to take each year—and that, of course, also means me practicing what I preach.

In any case, the job market for pilots will presumably change in the long run as a result of COVID-19. At the start of the year, the industry was still desperately looking for new pilots. A report published in 2019 expected a demand for more than 800,000 pilots until 2040. Then came the pandemic, which swiftly turned the entire industry on its head. Anyone who just had their hours cut, as opposed to losing their job, could consider themselves lucky. To make things even harder, a pilot is not a recognized trade in Germany. Many of us, myself included, thus currently face an uncertain future, having not completed any recognized apprenticeship. The years 2020 and 2021 presumably won't be good years for anyone to start training to be a pilot either. Anyone thinking of doing so should first wait for the industry to recover.

I believe and hope everything will look a lot better in two years' time than it does now.

Aviation should use this enforced break to take a hard look at itself. As I said earlier, diversity continues to be an alien concept in the cockpit. But it shouldn't be that difficult to appeal directly to women and members of minorities. A lack of diversity also means a lack of perspectives. Only three percent of all captains are women—and it was seriously six years before I myself finally flew with a female captain for the first time. In all my years as a pilot in European aviation, I have never encountered a person of color in the cockpit. Of course, not all pilots are like the old troopers who so often made my life more difficult than it needed to be. I have met many amazing, unbigoted colleagues, though most were from younger generations. But the fact that flying has for decades been considered a "man's job" has now made the cockpit a place that really struggles with change.

Dear aviation industry, you can do better. It's time ignorant comments about women and minorities became a thing of the past. Belittling others and putting yourself above them is never the right way to improve your own stature. I am totally optimistic about the capacity of old white men to learn. If we put them alongside lots of women, LGBTQ, and people of color in the cockpit, they'll eventually see that competence and authority are learnable skills—and not a privilege reserved for the so-called masters of creation.

For all the ill the virus has caused, COVID-19 could absolutely be a catalyst for more diversity in the cockpit. Once the industry has recovered, the lack of qualified female pilots will be all the more apparent. But let's not just be satisfied with a "wait and see"; the only thing that will drive us forward is a valiant "let's do this!"

I've built up a large and ever-growing follower base in recent years, and I wouldn't mind seeing it get even bigger. Over the last few years, even the traditional media—print and TV—have regularly been approaching me, and if this results in opportunities for projects that have nothing to do with aviation, then I'm open to suggestions! (My current dream is to be cast as the next James Bond. I can imagine doing a few spectacular air chases, with me doing the stunts myself. Plus, it's high time there was a Bond Boy. We could have a big casting show, and the winner at the end gets to play the role.)

CHAPTER

LISTEN, BABY!

Did you guys notice? The lists haven't been making much of an appearance. But I really am a fan of them. (A book, two coming-outs; yes, I do keep to-do lists.) But not to worry; I just wanted to finish with a few practical tips that are also available on my blog. Anyone who is as passionate about flying and who travels around the world as much as I do will learn, over the years, the best way to prepare themselves. Traveling well starts with the packing. As a private pilot, I've had the weirdest experiences when it comes to luggage. It is absolutely not uncommon for a single person to travel with eight suitcases. (We once loaded the entire cargo hold full of earthenware containers from Marrakech; some looked highly suspicious, and had me fearing the client might have been using them to dispose of disagreeable people.) But anyone who can't afford a private jet is of course advised to pack lighter. So here are my tips for aspiring pro packers:

Invest in a good suitcase. I swear by hard cases. You can get them in all different sizes, they protect your luggage excellently against knocks, and will help you keep things in order while away. For me, it is essential they have four wheels on the bottom and a handle on the top. For short trips, a hard case in carry-on format will usually suffice. For longer trips, a "big brother" can go along in the cargo hold.

What to pack in your carry-on luggage

- Passport (this is obvious)
- Camera (unless you take all your photos with a cell phone)
- Noise-canceling headphones (a blessing on long-haul flights)
- Tablet (for e-books, movies, social media etc.)
- Bluetooth soundbox (for listening to music and watching movies on your tablet in the hotel)
- Mobile charger (essential with all the hodgepodge of electronic devices)
- Shades (I personally prefer aviators—no idea where that would come from)
- Wallet (check again beforehand to make sure you really don't have more than US$10,000 in it)

Where possible, I put electronic devices in my carry-on luggage, just in case my checked luggage gets lost. A few T-shirts are easier and cheaper to replace than a tablet or camera. But check your airline's regulations for this beforehand.

What to pack in your checked luggage

- Clothes (I take simple but stylish items I can easily combine)
- Toiletries bag (I swear by organic toiletries; depending on your destination, don't forget sunscreen either!)
- A second pair of shoes (for me, it's the sneakers that are a must-take)

- Suspension trainer (a simple but supereffective gym tool that can be used anywhere)

Additional packing tips

- If your suitcase has inside pockets, use them for socks and underwear. After all, every cubic inch is precious.
- Valuables, passport, and other important documents go in your carry-on luggage (see above).
- If you're packing shirts, it is advisable to put them in individual cloth or, if need be, plastic bags. This keeps them smooth so they don't need to be re-ironed.
- Put your toiletries in a plastic bag. If something leaks while you're traveling, at least it won't mess up the rest of your suitcase.
- It is recommended to take travel-size cosmetics, perfumes, etc. This saves space. You can also buy small empty bottles and fill them with your products of choice before your trip.
- If you're taking a suit, I recommend a suit pack to prevent creases.
- The major airlines generally permit another small bag (such as a fanny pack or purse) in addition to regular hand luggage. This is a good place to keep your passport and cell phone.
- Always pack your suitcase the same way so you can quickly find what you're looking for.

- Your suitcase absolutely must be secured with a lock. Pros make sure they have a TSA lock. Some background info: If the luggage checks detect an unidentifiable object (or the detection dog starts barking), the luggage will, in cases of doubt, be opened by force. The advantage of a TSA lock is that security staff can open it with a Transportation Security Administration (in case you were wondering what the abbreviation stood for) master key without needing a number combination or the original key.

Ten tips to combat your fear of flying

You would think that, as a pilot, I wouldn't have too many followers who suffer from a fear of flying. But I have actually been asked repeatedly what people can do to combat this very fear. And as I, of course, don't just want to fob you guys off with a smug "don't fly," here are my ten tips to overcome your fear of flying:

1. Choose an airline with a good reputation and where you know you will be in safe hands. When a flight attendant on a budget carrier makes an onboard announcement asking if someone can change a 20-dollar bill, it doesn't exactly instill a lot of confidence. And you're better off buying raffle tickets at a funfair. Economizing on a plane ticket is a false economy.

2. Get to the airport on time; give yourself enough time for check-in and bag drop. Because stress will only make your fear worse. For long-haul flights, arriving two hours before departure is the absolute minimum.

3. If possible, book a seat with a little more leg room. Those who book early may be fortunate enough to snatch the seats right by the emergency exit, for example.

4. Ideally avoid drinking coffee or alcohol during the flight, as both could exacerbate your fear of flying.

5. There is absolutely no shame in letting the cabin crew know, when you board, that you are a little nervous. A brief conversation can calm your nerves, and a good flight attendant will try to ease your fear by taking extra care of you.

6. Always remember the air safety statistics. Statistically speaking, you are much, much more likely to win the jackpot in the lottery than to die in an air crash. (Hey, maybe you can buy that ticket after all, if you're able to break the twenty-dollar bill for the stewardess.)

7. Think about your breathing. Many people find it helpful to consciously inhale slowly through their nose an exhale through their mouth. Verrry slowly and relaxed.

8. Got your noise-canceling headphones in your carry-on? Great. Listen to a playlist of relaxing music to drown out the noise of the plane and people around you. Snacks, a good book, or an eye mask can also help you forget the world around you.

9. Always remember: You're not alone. Many thousands of people are in the air at the same time as you.

10. And finally, don't forget that planes are designed and built with the utmost care. Even though it may not feel like it, a little turbulence won't do anything to it or you.

On that note, *safe travels ... and happy landings!*

Pilot Patrick

About the author

Patrick Biedenkapp, better known as Pilot Patrick, has been a professional pilot since 2010. After flying business jets for nearly seven years, the 31-year-old Berliner-by-choice now flies for a major international airline. With more than 750,000 Instagram followers and over 150,000 YouTube subscribers, Pilot Patrick has become one of Germany's best-known airline captains.

Made in the USA
Las Vegas, NV
21 November 2020